JERRY PAM:

Memoirs of a Hollywood Publicist

JERRY PAM:

Memoirs of a Hollywood Publicist

with
Gareth Owen

BearManor Media
2017

Jerry Pam: Memoirs of a Hollywood Publicist

© 2017 Jerry Pam & Gareth Owen

All Rights Reserved.
Reproduction in whole or in part without the author's permission is strictly forbidden.

Gareth Owen
Pinewood Studios, Iver Heath, Bucks
SL0 0NH. UK
Tel: +44 1753 651700
gareth@mooreoffice.co.uk

BearManor Media
P. O. Box 71426
Albany, GA 31708

bearmanormedia.com

Typesetting and layout by John Teehan

Published in the USA by BearManor Media

ISBN—978-1-62933-139-3

Dedicated to my loving wife Janice and our children Lesley, Erin, Susan and Tim.

FOREWORD

by Sir Roger Moore

I FIRST MET JERRY in the MGM publicity department back in 1954 when, as a fresh faced young British actor, I was delighted to encounter a fellow Londoner; we soon became great friends.

When Jerry eventually left MGM to set up his own PR company, he became my personal publicist and remained so until we lost him to that great cutting room in the sky.

Jerry with Roger Moore, lifelong friends.

Jerry lived in a tiny house in Dick Street, in West Los Angeles, though always threw the biggest parties. It was very much an open house policy for his fellow ex-pats to drop in, and many was the time I arrived to see a cast of A-list actors that any producer would give his right arm to star in a movie! There was more box office at Jerry's house than in many of the studios combined.

Sadly, towards the end of his life, Jerry's extraordinary memory and knowledge of everything Hollywood was cruelly affected by illness, and our contact became more sporadic. However, a few months before he passed away, to my great surprise and delight, he called me up out of the blue and was very much the old Jerry I knew and loved. We chatted about everything and everyone. I'm so pleased our last conversation was such a happy one. I'm also so very pleased he committed many of his many memories and stories to this book, which is a fascinating insight into the world of the publicist and the many fascinating people he encountered throughout his career.

INTRODUCTION

by Gareth Owen

A NATIVE OF THE UK, JERRY PAM ventured to Hollywood in the 1950s to pursue the love of his life – movies.

He actually began his career in LA selling advertising space in *The Hollywood Reporter*, though his passion for film and showbiz soon saw him become an entertainment reporter for a Beverly Hills newspaper where he pulled off a number of coups which, ultimately, led to him being noticed by and invited to join MGM's publicity department.

Jerry's baptism into the world of Hollywood was both fast and formidable, and he found himself working with Howard Keel, Roger Moore, Johnny Green, Greer Garson, Clark Gable, Debbie Reynolds, James Stewart, Katharine Hepburn and Gene Kelly to name but a few.

After working within the studio system for a few years Jerry decided to spread his wings and go freelance, establishing Pam Public Relations and specializing in production and release publicity for movies, along with representing the personal media interests of a number of actors, producers, directors, and companies. His big leap into the spotlight came when he introduced the Beatles to the United States – handling the promotion of *A Hard Day's Night* and *Help!* as well as all their Los Angeles concerts.

Throughout the 1970s, Jerry added to his roster of clients with Michael Caine, Jaclyn Smith, and Robert Stack, in addition to writers such as Sidney Sheldon, Jackie Collins, Judith Krantz, and Morris West.

Through the 1980s, 1990s, and into the 2000s, Jerry was most celebrated for his Oscar PR campaigns. Titles such as *Last Tango in Paris*, *American Graffiti*, *The Conversation*, *Shampoo*, *Midnight Express*, *Apocalypse Now*, *Dick Tracy*, *Cinema Paradiso*, *Unforgiven*, *Life is Beautiful*, and *Shakespeare in Love* were all brought to the world's attention through his office. Working quietly behind the scenes, Jerry generated public awareness and ensured – through a combination of trade newspaper inter-

Jerry Pam at the movies, the place and medium he loved all his life.

views, photo calls, advertisements, and TV chat show appearances – that all Academy voters had an opportunity to see all the contenders. He knew his audience and always had an idea or two up his sleeve to draw their attention to a project!

In this career memoir Jerry offers us a peek into his time in Hollywood and, whilst never betraying any confidences, he speaks frankly about the great and the not so great.

His client list read like a who's who of the business, and because of that very fact we decided to approach this book as a literal A-Z of Hollywood.

Sadly, Jerry passed away in November 2014 after a short illness, but was determined his memoir should be completed and shared with movie lovers everywhere.

Some of the films represented by Jerry Pam in production or in release:

Against the Wall
Agnes of God
Amelia
American Graffiti
Apocalypse Now
Aviator, The
Barbarian Invasions, The
Brazil
Breezy
Bugsy
Chicago
China Syndrome, The
Chocolat
Cider House Rules, The
Cinema Paradiso
Cold Mountain
Conversation, The
Damien: Omen 2
Dick Tracy
Dirty Dozen, The
Educating Rita
Farewell My Lovely
Finding Neverland
Gangs of New York
Good Will Hunting
Gunfight, A
Hand, The
Hard Day's Night, A
Heaven Can Wait
Help!
Hero
High Road to China
Hugh Plains Drifter
Il Postino
In the Bedroom
Invincible Six, The
Iris
Killing of Sister George, The
Killing, The
Kolya

Last Tango in Paris
Les Choristes
Life Is Beautiful
Little Voice
Magnum Force
Man Who Would Be King, The
Man With One Red Shoe, The
Marty
Meteor
Midnight Express
Month by the Lake, A
Mouse on the Moon, The
Murder on the Orient Express
Night Watch
Omen, The
Paths of Glory
Quiet American, The
Reds
Seawolves, The
Scarecrow
Secret of Santa Vittoria, The
Shakespeare In Love
Shampoo
Shiner
Shipping News, The
Sunday Bloody Sunday
That Cold Day in the Park
The Greek Tycoon
Thousand Clowns, A
Tom and Viv
Too Late the Hero
Touch of Class, A
Town Without Pity, A
Twin Sisters
Unforgiven
Vanishing, The
White Hunter, Black Heart
Woman in Red, The
Year of Living Dangerously, The

SCENE 1

THE LUMINARIES OF HOLLYWOOD

IT WAS A BALMY EVENING in 1950s Beverly Hills as I made my way to the Salem House, a one-time fairly upscale restaurant located on what is known as Little Santa Monica Boulevard. I asked the maitre d' for a quiet table at the back of the well-lit dining room; it was imperative that I be seated away from other diners so as not to create disturbance. You see, I was about to interview a movie superstar.

After being seated at seven o'clock, our agreed meeting time, I waited and waited and waited. Two glasses of Bordeaux later, at 8:15pm, I saw diners looking up in disbelief and there was suddenly a distinct buzz of excitement in the room. Marilyn Monroe had arrived with her 20th Century Fox publicist Roy Kraft leading the way.

It was a huge feather in my cap to have secured Miss Monroe for an exclusive interview in my newspaper, *The Beverly Hills Citizen*, for which I was the entertainment editor. What they didn't know was I lived opposite Roy Kraft and he owed me a favour – and this was me calling it in!

The biggest surprise of the evening was still to come, though. Roy said he had to attend a Fox studio

Meeting Marilyn Monroe and my newspaper interview with her launched my career into an exciting new direction.

preview of a just-completed movie that evening, and asked if I was comfortable conducting the interview on my own.

Was I?! It was a dream come true – I had one of the world's most beautiful women all to myself for the better part of two hours.

We discussed everything from her career to her problems coping with private demons, her continued lateness, her studying Stanislavsky at the Actor's Studio, and why she famously kept the press waiting at Kennedy airport by delaying her departure off the plane. It was pure gold dust to this writer!

For the record

For many years my friends, acquaintances, clients, and even fellow publicists have enjoyed listening to some of my tales of Hollywood. They've all said at one time or another, "you should write a book, Jerry". I've smiled, nodded and said "yeah, yeah, one day".

It was when my daughter Lesley said she still has no idea what I *really* do for a living that I realised I couldn't give her a simple answer. I started telling her about some of the people I have known and worked with as a publicist, and my role in promoting them, their projects, and in sometimes not promoting them – keeping certain news stories *out* of the papers! Lesley couldn't quite believe how lucky I'd been, and that was a real eye-opening moment, because until that point I'd never sat back and thought about it. It was a job, and a job I loved, but wow I even surprised myself!

So, I thought I might write some stories down as a reminder, and maybe even a prompter for when I needed an after-dinner anecdote. However, the series of brief jottings and notes grew to pages, chapters, and eventually into a manuscript. It was then I thought about the "you should write a book, Jerry" comments.

Those I have known

I have been very fortunate to have met, known, and befriended a great many memorable people who have all left their mark on my psyche: The Beatles, Michael Caine, Roger Moore, Noel Coward, Robert Stack, Clint Eastwood, Warren Beatty, Glenda Jackson, Billy Wilder, Steven Spielberg, Judy Garland, and Ingrid Bergman to mention a few, have all been, in some way, responsible for shaping my career. Whether I represented them as a publicist individually, or in film projects, or perhaps even as a young journalist, I have now tried to remember people, places, and events as best I can.

I might add this is not a "kiss and tell biography." As a publicist I have often been entrusted with confidential information by a client and would never betray that trust.

There are many terms used in Hollywood for the job I do, ranging from "publicity" and "public relations" to "exploitation" and "marketing," but basically it all comes down to creating a positive awareness of the person, motion picture, TV show, musical event, record, CD, DVD, ad infinitum. The key message being, "to achieve a continuity of stories and photographs extolling the virtues of the product."

As a journalist, I began to realize how creative press agents were by the presentations they submitted. When I made the decision to join their ranks I realized if I was ever going to succeed amid the great competition, I'd have to work twice as hard as anyone else – but hard work has never scared me.

I hope, in some small way, the following pages will inspire those who have aspirations like I did to reach for the stars and make their dreams come true.

The big problem in writing a book is, of course, knowing where to begin – and not be too boring. It's probably a good idea to tell you first how I got started!

SCENE 2

EARLY BEGINNINGS

I WAS BORN IN 1926 IN LONDON. My childhood was quite wonderful, and though I was an only child and, admittedly, sometimes felt lonely, my mum and dad soon put pay to those thoughts by telling me I was their love child and all the more special for it. This was undoubtedly the basis of my very happy formative years. My parents worked hard to enable me to enjoy a good education, and I will be forever grateful to them for that.

Aged 10 I entered Hackney Downs Grammar School (also known as the "Worshipful Company of Grocers") just a few years before World War II broke out in Europe. Little did I realize I would soon be one of thousands of evacuees being shipped away to the countryside, far away from the big towns which were nightly bombing-targets for the Luftwaffe.

For six years I was billeted with a family in King's Lynn, Norfolk, and although I travelled on vacations to see my parents, who had since moved to Northampton, I relished the way of life within the farming community – not to mention plentiful fresh eggs, milk, and cream.

One of my great joys was travelling to the local cinema to escape in the world of movies for a couple of hours – in fact, I often went three times a week! I had a particularly voracious appetite for Hollywood escapism and could never really get enough of it. My thirst was unquenchable. It was like being plunged into a wonderful fantasy land for an hour or two, dreaming of being far away from the war and into a lifestyle I so envied.

Because of restrictions placed on youngsters seeing more "adult" orientated films, I would often walk down the length of the queue outside the cinema and ask a kindly-looking grown up to take me in, and gave him my sixpence admission.

Clark Gable, Spencer Tracy, and Humphrey Bogart became my big screen idols, but I never for one moment thought that one day I would meet all three!

As the years rolled by I lapped up most of America's best, along with European sub-titled features, and of course British productions. But it was the Hollywood films that captivated me most. I believed that if I could one day, somehow, get to the United States, then I was, without doubt, destined to be a part of this magical medium.

Foolish childhood aspirations? Day dreams? Call it what you will, but the seeds were very much sown: the world of movies, and Hollywood, was for me.

Following school, meanwhile, I was drafted into the army for National Service and spent two ridiculous years performing various guard duties. I say ridiculous because the war was over, there was no real threat of another conflict starting, and the armed-services had tens of thousands of us with nothing to do apart from march, practice guard duty, and paint stones white. Thankfully I was rescued from this mundane life of service when selected to lead intelligence tests at a "Future Officers' Training Camp." It entailed training and testing cadets in the permanent army who showed potential to be commissioned officers, and it all really made my army life more pleasant – giving a real purpose to it. Upon demobilization, I went to university with thoughts of becoming a psychiatrist. I guess I'd become a good listener to all the trainee cadets and their problems? It was a long way removed from Hollywood, but seemed the obvious choice at the time.

I soon flopped in my medical ambitions however, when I became squeamish viewing an operation! I quickly changed to a journalism course, which was the best thing I could have done.

Upon graduation I landed a temporary job in Paris with the *Continental Daily Mail*. The editor seemed to get a kick out of sending me to interview Picasso, as they had tried for ages to speak with the great artist without any success. Maybe he thought a young, enthusiastic novice stood a better chance? Little did I know I was to be the latest in a long line of idiots they'd sent on the wild goose chase.

I duly left for the south of France to search for the elusive painter. I guess luck and timing were on my side, as I received a tip that he was in Vallauris, a suburb of Cannes. With my limited expenses dwindling, even before I'd arrived there, I realized it had to be a now or never approach – I had to go in with all guns blazing. I obtained the address of his small cha-

Pablo Picasso famously never gave interviews. I didn't know that before I set off to interview him!

teau from a local shopkeeper and continually rang the old-fashioned bell on the rusty gate which lead to his estate.

My high school French seemed to strike a chord with a manservant who eventually answered, and he asked me to wait. A few minutes later a giant of a man appeared and motioned me to come into the garden, pointing to a bench under an apple tree. After about 20 minutes, the bronze coloured painter himself approached from the house and silently ushered me into his studio. It contained so many paintings that I felt I was back in Paris' famed Louvre.

He expressed in no uncertain terms that he did not give interviews, then picked up a marking pencil and started to sketch on a canvas. I saw he had drawn my head protruding from a block of wood! There was no conversation aside from a curt "au revoir" and I was led out of his atelier to be met by the giant, who escorted me off the property.

I returned to Paris to face a furious editor. Not only had I failed to get an interview, I could offer no photo to back up my story of meeting the great man at his home, being invited into his studio, and him sketching me. It all sounded a bit far-fetched I admit, but it was true. My employment was nevertheless terminated – my temporary job proved to be very temporary indeed!

A life down-under

I then secured a not-too exciting job in London working in a cuckoo clock factory. It was 1950 and London was recovering from the war, rationing was still in force and it was a pretty depressing time with no real prospects.

My parents decided that the family should emigrate to Australia. Dad's brother, my Uncle Charles, had already settled there and loved it. From being regarded as "the continent that time forgot," Australia was keen to now sell itself as "the land of opportunity"; all this was when England was recovering from its lowest ebb. My mother suffered with rheumatoid arthritis and was told a warmer climate would be beneficial, and so we made plans to move to the new world.

Whilst Australia had many things in common with England, a shared language being one, it was also in many respects a total contrast

Moulin Rouge, the film that changed my life.

to the depressed country we'd left; the sun was always shining, food was plentiful, and there seemed to be a sense of great hope and aspiration. I liked it hugely.

Of course, matters soon turned to employment – I needed some! My first job was with a company that specialized in food and health products – Reckitt and Colman – including everything from antiseptics to mustard. Who knew that had health benefits?! My role was to analyze advertising placements for all their products, and also to ensure all print ads were correct and submitted to publications in time to meet deadlines. I did this for about six months until I moved sideways into advertising sales for health trade magazines, whom I'd actually got to know through taking adverts for Reckitt and Colman. It was certainly well paid, but totally uninspiring – being on the telephone eight hours a day trying to sell space did not enthuse me one bit! A year or so after arriving in the great land of opportunity I realised I needed to make a decision on where my life was heading.

Meanwhile, my hack skills, first developed at my (brief) sojourn at the *Mail* in Paris, proved useful in securing me a few film-related writing assignments for magazines and a newspaper in Sydney. My great appetite for Hollywood escapism was well-sustained too, with all I could lap up. In fact it was seeing one film that changed my entire outlook on life and my career, such as it was. John Huston's *Moulin Rouge* captivated me like no other: its magnificent recreation of late 19th century Paris which transported me back in time so faithfully was a Pandora's box to me. I realized just how powerful and persuasive a medium film was.

This was my epiphany. I knew my future lay in films – how and where remained to be seen though.

The way in.

Then in 1952 I saw a chance! I was invited to an advance screening of *Kangaroo*, which starred Maureen O'Hara, Peter Lawford, and Richard Boone. It was, to say the least, a pretty poor Australian-set romantic adventure, and one which certainly didn't show the country in a good light. I decided to write a letter to Spyros P. Skouras, the president of Twentieth Century Fox, highlighting his company's embarrassing and ill-thought out depiction of my lovely new home, and how I felt it would be PR suicide for them to ride into town on the back of it – as I knew Skouras was due to land in Sydney for the premiere of the movie within weeks. I wanted him to know his reception might not be all he hoped for.

Looking back, I can see how easily I, a jumped-up young hack telling a studio head that the movie he had commissioned wasn't going to be well received, could have so easily been ignored or disregarded in a "who the hell does he think he is?" waive of Skouras' powerful hand. But imagine my surprise when Mr Skouras' personal secretary contacted me to fix a meeting with his employer! He furthermore explained there was to be a press briefing two days later at the Hotel Australia and said that he needed somebody who could help them avoid any pointed criticism and, in particular, any awkward questions about Australia, as depicted in *Kangaroo*. They had a movie to open, and weren't keen on the critics sinking it without them having at least a chance of recouping some of their budget. Skouras was conscious of the facts but needed a diversion that would 1) be newsworthy and 2) deflect the worst criticism of the movie. He was, in short, looking for a fall guy, and I walked right into the frame.

If I accepted this assignment, he said he would offer me a fee five times my weekly stipend.

I realized it could be the start of a very exciting new chapter in my life – here I was meeting the president of a Hollywood studio, the very place I wanted to work. I also knew all too well that if I messed up I would be dropped like a lead balloon, and be a convenient excuse for the film's misfiring. It was a chance of a lifetime; how could I not take it up?

But, equally, how could I shift the focus of the press conference away from Fox's big release in Australia? It was an Australian subject and that is all the national press would want to talk about – or rip apart. I ferociously looked around for ammunition and found it in film trade newspaper *Variety* – Fox had just announced the casting of Gregory Peck and Ava Gardner in a new African adventure *The Snows of Kilimanjaro*.

As the press conference commenced, several mem-

With Spyros Skouras, head of 20th Century Fox.

bers of the assembled media naturally started shouting questions out awkwardly about *Kangaroo*. I realized this was my moment to take the bull by the horns. Climbing onto the top table where the famed Fox executive was sitting I shouted out:

"Gentlemen, Mr Skouras was not here during filming, and so may be unable to answer many of your queries. I am confident, though, that he will be able to reveal exclusive information regarding Fox's forthcoming production in Africa with two of our biggest screen stars."

The journalists took the bait and Skouras was more than delighted to talk about anything other than *Kangaroo*.

He later suggested, for a similar fee, that I might like to organize a dinner for the Greek Orthodox community of New South Wales to honour one of the most famous Greeks in the world – him! He was nothing if immodest.

I duly obliged and the dinner attracted a record crowd, all paying homage (and a hefty attendance fee) to Mr Skouras.

In turn, he not only gave me a huge bonus for both events, but also offered me a position in the Hollywood studio's publicity department. Hollywood!

My initial elation and excitement soon turned to a more realistic thought of upheaval. Having just laid the foundations for a new life down under, there would be another move across the world, and away from my parents. Further underlining my ties to Australia was my fiancé Diana, and she was emphatic – we were not moving anywhere, and that was that.

I sadly couldn't accept Skouras' offer then, at any rate, and continued my life having to be content with just writing about movies. At the back of my mind there was a constant niggle; had I just turned down my one and only chance to work at one of the powerhouses of Los Angeles? That, after all, was where my spirit had always been, and opportunities like that don't happen very often.

I found myself, for the first time since arriving, thoroughly unhappy and depressed. I liked Australia greatly but I felt that the country's film industry was a poor relation to everywhere else in the world, so much so I knew I'd never again have a chance to work at the heart of a thriving movie business.

I couldn't help but recall Ava Gardner, when in Melbourne to shoot *On the Beach*, based on the Neville Shute book, commenting to a reporter who asked her why she was there

"I am here to star in a movie about the end of the world – and they have picked the right place to film it."

In the short, miserable time after turning the job down, I knew just what a mistake I'd made. I phoned Fox to see if Mr Skouras' offer might still stand, and explained about how my initial decision had been a mistake. To my delight, they said there was still a job if I wanted it. Diana, meanwhile, didn't want to go, but I told her that with or without her, I was now going.

Thankfully, and probably seeing I was deadly serious, she agreed to join me on my new adventure. We decided it was the perfect moment to get married, and seven days later sailed on the SS Lakemba for Vancouver, via Fiji.

Hollywood beckons.

Despite questions from our families of how could we travel to a foreign country where we had no friends, no relatives, and only knew the president of Twentieth Century Fox, it seemed like we'd made the right decision. It all just felt right.

Once we reached Los Angeles I presented myself at the studios and noticed just one car in the gigantic parking lot – a pure white 1953 Cadillac convertible. I thought it must have been a holiday as there was nobody to be seen anywhere.

I found the personnel office, but was horrified (to put it mildly) when the secretary informed me that most of the staff had just been dismissed and movie production had been shut down indefinitely. There had, she told me, been a major drop in cinema attendance due to the new, competing method of entertainment – television. I pulled out the photograph of me with Skouras in Australia and explained how much he wanted me to work for him, and that I'd travelled half way around the world to be there. The astonished secretary made a few phone calls and I was then escorted into the office of the studio's head of production, Darryl F. Zanuck. He proceeded to give me a fifteen-minute summary of the problems facing Hollywood. It was eye-opening, as was their planned way of reclaiming cinema-goers:

"All the Hollywood studios are feeling the impact of TV," he said. "And at this moment, we are experimenting in our Western Avenue studio with a new anamorphic lens called CinemaScope. If this is successful, we will revolutionize the industry in much the same way as when sound was introduced".

Up to this time all films were projected in a ratio of 1.33 to one, and Fox was funding experiments in expanding this to a wide screen format – to really offer a big screen experience that TV simply couldn't compete with.

CinemaScope's anamorphic lens would indeed be Fox's revolutionary contribution to the industry, and its first widescreen feature was the biblical drama *The Robe*.

After his pronouncement, Zanuck concluded our meeting with "We recognize the difficult situation in which you find yourself and may be able to assist you in the foreseeable future, just not now."

Job hunting

I left his office feeling very disillusioned. Waiting for *The Robe* to be released later that year would not put bread on the table; so I started pounding the streets looking for a position.

Having married in Sydney, this period was supposed to be our honeymoon. Some honeymoon! Here we were alone in a new country, trying to fathom a new language – American. George Bernard Shaw wrote that the British and the Americans were divided by a common language. How right he was.

I raised many eyebrows when I wanted cookies and called them biscuits; an eraser was known back home as a rubber; and to call on friends was NOT to knock them up. I soon learned that being English had its drawbacks.

But we were in LA and had to try and make a go of things before our meagre savings were all used up. So I continued to knock on doors.

My persistence eventually paid off when, in the summer of '53, I was hired by *The Hollywood Reporter*, a noted trade paper, to sell advertising on a commission basis. I would receive 15% on any sales and was assigned two studios, Republic and Universal. Little did I realize that they had suspended all advertising due to the crisis of TV competition!

The only saving grace was that I was also allowed to solicit advertising for real estate sales, whose one inch ads cost $8. Billy Wilkerson, the paper's owner, was fascinated when he regularly handed me checks for $6.80 and $13.60.

"Why would you stay here for such slim pickings?" He asked. Slim pickings to him, but food on the table to me!

The paper's advertising manager, Jack Hadley, took pity on me and suggested that I approach the *Beverly Hills Citizen*, a daily newspaper. There seemed to be an advertising position available which paid no commissions, but the astronomical salary of $80 per week.

Thank goodness I must have made a good impression in the interview, as I was hired on the spot. To my amazement, the job also included journalistic work on the entertainment beat. I was so enthused that on my first day I sold a full year's advertising contract for Cinerama, and at the same time commenced writing a gossip column, reviewing movies and theatre and covering the few nightclubs in town.

My dream to be part of the Hollywood scene had finally come to fruition, albeit not quite the way I'd anticipated when I boarded that ship in Sydney!

SCENE 3

THE LION'S ROAR

WITHIN A YEAR OF JOINING THE PAPER I moved away from the cut and thrust of selling advertising space to become more and more involved in writing entertainment features and stories. I loved it.

My enthusiasm was evident to see and I must have impressed someone, as I was invited to become the entertainment editor.

I presumed that I would write movie reviews, a gossip column, and conduct interviews with stars on the sets of their movies. Little did I realize that I would soon be called up and schmoozed by publicists trying to plant stories of their various clients on my entertainment page.

You see, in 1953 there were five metropolitan daily newspapers in LA: the *Los Angeles Times*, *Mirror*, *Herald-Express*, *Examiner*, and *Daily News*. The *Daily News* was about to disappear though, and publicists realized that a very valuable one-fifth of their available print exploitation was going with it. That's when the three main suburban dailies, the *Hollywood Citizen-News*, the *Valley Times*, and the *Beverly Hills Citizen* suddenly grew in importance. If a publicist failed to get a story into the big four, these newspapers could come to their rescue. I suddenly became important to the Hollywood players!

I was often wined and dined and became friends with many of the studio publicists. It was a dream job for a movie-mad hack.

A little too risqué

Walter Shenson, a charming representative of Columbia Studios, came into my office one morning. He became a semi-regular visitor, presenting stories and/or photos for publication in the paper. On this visit

Full use of the horizontal was made on the poster!

he convinced me to publish a photograph of Burt Lancaster and Deborah Kerr lying very romantically on a beach in Hawaii. "This is an exclusive," he emphasized, meaning that no other publication would print before me.

I should have suspected something was afoot as here I was, on a modest neighbourhood newspaper, being offered something one of the big LA newspapers always had first option on. Nevertheless, I ran with the photograph, which of course was from the epic movie *From Here to Eternity*, and was duly very nearly fired!

The managing editor summoned me, after the first edition the following morning, and demanded to know why I had used a "horizontal." I hadn't the faintest idea what he was talking about until he explained that this was a family newspaper and it was taboo to have a man lying on top of a woman in a romantic setting.

It turned out that Shenson had a bet with his boss, Harry Cohn (the head of Columbia Pictures), that he would get the photograph printed in a LA newspaper, and of course all the others had turned him down.

I later received a phone call from Shenson, full of apologies, which ended with a promise that he owed me a major favor. More on that a little later.

MGM

Landing my aforementioned interview with Marilyn Monroe certainly earned me extra brownie points at the newspaper and, unbeknownst to me, also got me noticed at MGM.

One day in early 1954 Howard Strickling called and asked if I would be interested in joining his publicity department at Metro-Goldwyn-Mayer Studios.

I didn't need to think about it!

After accepting the offer, I received a call from possibly the most important newspaper woman in the country, the legendary Louella Parsons, with another offer. She planned to enter the TV arena and needed an assistant – immediately. She said that Harry Brand, head of publicity at Fox studios, had recommended me. When I explained that I had just committed to MGM, Louella replied, "Don't worry, I know Howard extremely well and he will do what I say. After all I created the headline which MGM uses all the time – 'Hollywood Is Talking About'…"

Within a week, Parsons was taken ill and the TV deal was cancelled, along with any opportunity for me working for her. I had, however, been quite astute and decided not to say anything to MGM until my contract with Louella Parsons arrived. So, MGM knew nothing about it and their job offer still stood.

I packed up my desk at the newspaper, and although happy to be leaving for MGM, I knew the great debt I owed them all in giving me a big leg up in my career. I never forgot it either.

With Howard Strickling who gave me the chance to join MGM Studios' publicity department.

I next reported to MGM's studio in Culver City for my first day and my first meeting with the heads of the various publicity and advertising departments. These 60 men and women, the lifeblood of MGM's gigantic promotion apparatus, were all assigned actors, directors, producers, composers, etc. – all of whom were under contract to the

Howard Keel (here with Ava Gardner).

studio. I was told to arrange meetings with those assigned to me – Howard Keel, Roger Moore, Johnny Green, Fernando Lamas, Arthur Freed, and Jack Cummings. I was to "do their bidding." As I had seen Howard Keel in *Annie Get Your Gun* on the London stage, I decided to introduce myself to him first. It would be a good opening to our conversation if nothing else.

"Hello Harold" I said, and he immediately corrected me with "Howard". He was startled to think that I didn't know his screen name, but I explained that I had seen him on stage in London where he was billed as Harold. After a tense minute or so – when I thought I might have blown it on my first day! – he explained that he had since changed his name in America, and did not want it revealed to the public. I promised that I of course would not mention it, but the press did discover his name change as soon as he became a major star. What a star he became too!

Though after his contract with MGM ended he, like many other former contract players, had to accept some rather questionable films in order to pay the rent. But he happily became a household name again in the 80s thanks to the tv series *Dallas*, in which he played Harold ... sorry, I mean Clayton Farlow.

Nepotism

Producer Jack Cummings had the fortune – or misfortune – of being the nephew of MGM boss Louis B. Mayer. His motion pictures were varied and went from the dramatic to the heart of the studios' background musicals. He had just produced a musical drama based on the life of the Australian diva Marjorie Lawrence who, in spite of being stricken with polio, made one of the great comebacks in operatic history.

Jack took me into his sumptuous office and let me see a letter that had just arrived from a member of the public. With tears in our eyes we read how a New Yorker housewife had lost her husband to a fatal disease and decided that life was no longer worth living. She described what was to be her last day on earth, walking through Central Park and the various avenues with which she was most familiar. On passing a cinema she noticed the film *Interrupted Melody* was playing. It was "the true story of Marjorie Lawrence's triumph over adversity," starring Eleanor Parker, Glenn Ford, and Roger Moore.

Deciding to spend her last hours with one final movie, she entered the theatre, and two hours later came out crying. The inspiration she drew from the Australian diva's resolve to appear in public and perform on stage from a wheelchair motivated the would-be suicide victim to change her mind.

Cummings urged me to release the letter to the media, emphasizing that of all the films he had produced, this was the first occasion on which he had felt the power of a movie; and how it had constructively triumphed on many levels – not least in its entertainment value.

Keeping it out of the papers

I might add at this point that while the publicist's job was to primarily create an awareness of a film or a client, there are sometimes situations where one has to protect him/her against adverse stories – whether they be true or false. Preserving relationships and reputations is terribly important. One example being when Lana Turner got drunk at a nightclub in a seedy part of Los Angeles.

Upon hearing this, Howard Strickling immediately assigned some of his veteran publicists to see that she arrived home without incident. If the police were called the studio would have hushed up the event and the press would be circumvented. Today this would make headlines in papers across the country, and also be reported on social media instantly.

The main function of any studio publicist was in being responsible for the daily output of stories, which would then be utilized to promote the movie both during filming and in advance of release. A stills photographer, working under the supervision of the publicist, would also be assigned to cover the major scenes, and a daily set of black & white and colour proofs would be produced. These would then be shown to any of the film's stars with contracts for photo approval, who would in turn exclude those they felt unflattering.

At some point during production a "portrait gallery" sitting would be organized. This was mainly for headshots of the artists together with suggested advertising art, for posters and advertisements. The publicist would then be required to caption all the proofs for final selection.

Daily visits to the set were mandatory, to collect news, and at the same time gather information needed for any features and biographies, simply by chatting with the individuals in question.

Interviews with the media were usually arranged for just before lunch, so as the journalist could observe some filming and then adjourn for a meal in the nearby commissary or restaurant – all at the studio's expense, naturally. The publicist would usually be in attendance for two reasons: 1) to assist and control the theme of discussion so that the movie remained the main topic, and 2) to pay for lunch!

During the course of production, the publicist was required to write a press kit consisting of biographies of the principal actors, a synopsis of the plot, and any relevant feature stories that could be syndicated.

Nowadays, this would also include an electronic press kit (EPK) containing on-camera interviews, behind the scenes snippets, as well as showcasing a few important scenes from the finished product.

A constant feed via telephone, print, and photos was also supplied to columnists on the two Hollywood trade papers, *Daily Variety* and the *Hollywood Reporter*, along with the important New York, Chicago, and Los Angeles daily newspapers.

MGM had long been recognized by its slogan "All The Stars That Are in the Heavens." Unfortunately, I arrived at the end of the great contract era, but sitting in the commissary one could still observe Greer Garson, the one and only "King" Clark Gable, Debbie Reynolds, Jimmy Stewart, Katharine Hepburn, Gene Kelly, and many others dining. Being the largest studio at that time, there were always 5 or 6 films being produced at any one time so there was never any shortage of talent on the lot.

Roger Moore.

The studio also boasted the most charming of gatekeepers, and one in particular rejoiced in his real name – Kenny Hollywood. He knew every employee by sight and name and was a good friend to the press, as when journalists drove onto the lot he would impart the latest news of which stars were working and where – he was a good ally to the publicity department as, of course, we could feed him little stories to give the visiting media!

Moving on

As happy as I was during my couple of years working at MGM, my life changed with the arrival of my daughter Lesley in November 1955. I recognized that additional responsibilities required additional resources, and the studio couldn't offer me a raise.

I felt I'd reached a crossroads in my life. Yes, I'd gained very valuable experience, contacts, and insight at MGM, but the studio system was dying, and rates of pay would largely be the same anywhere else as at MGM, even if I could get my foot in the door.

The only way forward, I believed, was now to become an independent publicist and take on clients, films, and projects as they came along. I certainly wouldn't get rich working for someone, but I might earn a few more bucks working for myself.

With this in mind, I departed on very amicable terms and established my own publicity office. My first clients were Roger Moore, Marie Windsor, and a nightclub based at the former Earl Carroll's theatre in Hollywood, called The Moulin Rouge.

SCENE 4

GOING INDEPENDENT

Fortunately, my spell at MGM Studios gave me some decent credentials, having worked with many stars and, as publicist, quite a few films, including massive hits *Seven Brides for Seven Brothers* and *Bad Day at Black Rock*. I felt confident that I would be able to handle any project that came my way – well, that's called chutzpah.

Having spread the word that I was available for hire amongst all my friends and contacts, I was offered a film. It was a Pine-Thomas-Shane drama, *Nightmare*, which starred Edward G. Robinson, Kevin McCarthy, and Connie Russell.

The action took place in New Orleans with musician, McCarthy, involved in a bizarre murder. All the stars were incredibly amenable in cooperating for publicity, and as soon as it was ready to be launched on the world I organised a big press lunch featuring a New Orleans jambalaya meal. Okay, it may not have been the best film of the year but it was well made, had a good cast, and made a profit for the backers.

Edward G. Robinson was a favorite of the newspaper world and was at his best revealing that "Crime Does Pay" – so far as his career was concerned. He invested 25% of his income in fine impressionist art and his collection was regarded as the finest outside any museum.

A few years later I was invited to his Beverly Hills home to view his entire collection, not as a social engagement but in my publicist capacity, as he needed to sell them and raise awareness of the sale. You see his (soon to be) ex-wife was due a share of the Renoirs, Monet's, and Lautrec's in an impending divorce.

Eddie drew up a list of every piece and asked his wife to tick off the paintings that she wanted. He did likewise and where they did NOT co-

With Edward G Robinson.

incide they each agreed to keep them. The balance was sold at auction. How civilized!

My luck was in

A couple of other assignments also followed, including work on *Written on the Wind*, which starred Robert Stack and *The Killing* with Marie Windsor. All in all, my gambit of going freelance seemed to be paying off.

And 50 years later I was still doing pretty much the same job – so I'd like to think I did something right.

In that ensuing half-century I worked with a huge number of people on both sides of the camera and on over 75 movies. My involvement would be as diverse as looking after a visiting star on the promotion trail, handling movie launches, thinking up Oscar campaigns, and looking after the interests of a number of long-time clients with the odd "can you keep this out of the media?" panic request thrown in.

In fact, looking back it is quite daunting to see all the names, places, and films listed in my diaries, and I wondered just how I might collate them in the rest of this memoir. Then it came to me! I'd often been told by friends that I had worked with a veritable A-Z of Hollywood … so why not that?

THE A TO Z

What follows is my collection of memories, anecdotes, facts, and observations from my career as a Hollywood publicist.

A

ACADEMY OF MOTION PICTURE ARTS AND SCIENCES (AMPAS)

It is fortuitous that the Academy should be the first entry, as it is the Academy that really dominated my life and career.

As a publicist it is my job to raise awareness of films and, hopefully, steer them towards the ultimate goal – that of winning one of the Academy's prized statuettes, an Oscar.

I have been a member of the Academy since the 1960s, though remain amazed that such a high-profile body (how many hundreds of millions tune in to the Awards show every February?) has very little public awareness about it, its history, and workings. Sure, everyone knows about the Oscars, but the awards are only a small part of the Academy's function.

Founded in 1927 by actor Douglas Fairbanks Sr., its first president, the Academy's aim was to honor achievements in one or more areas of production, with a coveted statuette. Although the award categories have changed throughout the years, some added and some eliminated, today there are 25 annual awards, plus testimonials and special awards, that are presented.

Members are invited to join. One cannot apply. The Academy and its members seek to advance the arts and sciences of motion pictures, including cooperation on technical advances in research and improvement of methods and equipment. AMPAS also provides a forum and meeting place for various branches and crafts. They foster educational activities between the professional community and the public at large.

Of course, the annual Oscar ceremony is still the highlight of the year's activity and contributes, via the highly rated network tv special, to the finances of the Academy, allowing members to view films all year round, utilize research facilities, and finance the student film awards which showcase unknown talent from around the world.

To filmmakers, winning a prized Oscar does much – from increasing box office revenue, increasing asking prices, improving negotiation for future projects, and opening many more new doors. It is also the ultimate accolade: the one thing that every filmmaker would love.

It's my job to try and make that happen!

Little old me on the red carpet at the Oscars.

AGAINST THE WALL
Feature film (1994)

I first met John Frankenheimer when he engaged me to represent this HBO-produced cable tv movie in 1994. I was, of course, very familiar with his work – which invariably reflected his deep concern for social, political, and philosophical issues. *The Birdman Of Alcatraz* dealt with prison reform issues; *Seven Days In May* with the anatomy of a military coup in Washington, D.C.; *The Manchurian Candidate* involved brainwashing and global intrigue; and *Black Sunday* confronted international terrorism.

Against the Wall was set against the 1971 Attica riots, and was filmed in the old Tennessee State Prison, which was actually remodelled for authenticity. The post-riot scenes are as exciting as anything the director has ever staged in his career.

He was a fascinating character to talk with and observe, and I remember during pre-production he turned to me and said:

"I have learned a great deal from Alfred Hitchcock, and am a strong believer in elaborate pre-production preparation. I put in an enormous creative effort long before the cameras start turning, and go over every physical detail of the project with a fine-tooth comb to ensure accuracy and the 'right feel' for each scene."

In one of the interviews I arranged to promote the movie, a journalist asked him how involved he was with casting.

"That is 60% of directing" he replied, "and one searches meticulously for the best talent to fill each role, giving full attention to each and every one. Once secured, I rehearse with the cast until I am satisfied they are ready and every 'take' will count as the camera starts rolling."

I learned a great deal from John Frankenheimer. So many directors turn up on set and haven't the first idea what is going to happen. He knew to the finest detail, and that shows on screen.

AGNES OF GOD
Feature film. (1985)

Columbia Pictures engaged me to handle the Oscar campaign on this movie directed by Norman Jewison, as they felt it one of their best productions of the year, and felt it worthy enough to spend a lot of money in lobbying the AMPAS members for their vote. I hadn't been involved with the movie during its production, but had read about it in the trade papers.

It dealt with a very sensitive subject involving a nun and whether she gave birth to a baby who was subsequently strangled. Norman knew that it would have to be handled carefully and thoughtfully if they were to stand a chance of nomination, as there was every chance it could backfire on us if it seemed we were trying to cash in on a tragic real life occurence.

In the event, three nominations were secured – Anne Bancroft for 'Best Actress', Meg Tilly for 'Supporting Actress', and George Delerue for 'Best Score'.

Unfortunately, the competition was tough that year and the nominations didn't turn into statuettes. However, just to be nominated really is an achievement and honor – it's not necessarily about winning the race, but being in it.

There isn't always a great deal to tell when one is engaged for just a few weeks on a project, as rarely do you get to meet the actors, except at the occasional junket or pre-Oscar lunch. I love this type of work, though – it is the publicist at his most creative!

ALDRICH, ROBERT
Director, Producer & Writer

I spent some years working with this wonderful filmmaker in the 1960s and '70s, and it was one of the most rewarding experiences of my professional career. The thing I most admired about Aldrich was that he was no hypocrite. He was always in search of finance for his films but would not compromise his integrity to obtain it. He was a very ethical man.

During the filming of the Kim Novak-Peter Finch drama *The Legend of Lylah Clare* in 1967, I received a phone call from MGM publicity head Howard Strickling, who told me that New York Governor Nelson Rockefeller and his wife were planning a trip to the studio where we were filming; and he said they would like to visit the set. To my horror, Aldrich said "Over my dead body … and if he shows up I am off."

What I subsequently discovered was they were first cousins and, by all accounts, the Rockefeller family said they would support Robert financially in any endeavour except the entertainment industry – the very one he wanted to become involved with. Now here they were requesting a visit to his movie set!

Needless to say, the visit never materialized!

Another time I observed his acting true to form was when he was in some financial difficulties and he agreed to direct a movie – away from his own company – purely to bring in a pay check. It was the Korean war project *Inchon*. After conducting a bit of research on the producer, Aldrich discovered he was one of the heads of the Korean "Moonie" religious cult. He immediately turned the picture down, refusing to be associated with the organization. His integrity once again was paramount, with no room to compromise – despite him needing the money. Former Bond director Terence Young ultimately directed the film, but it was to be one of the last of his career, and I must admit, it was pretty bad.

Robert's sense of humor was terrific, never more so than when we used to get together after a day's filming for a social drink and chat. Conversation often revolved around what was going on in the business and who was doing what to whom. He loved hearing all the gossip and very often supplied some juicy anecdotes he'd heard elsewhere. He even had a lookout window in his office at the studio where he would people watch, and observe what was happening on the downstairs soundstage. He particularly loved me to give him news and information before it appeared in the daily trade papers.

On set with Robert Aldrich

He became a "movie mogul" after having had a rather good run of hits such as *Vera Cruz*(1954), *Whatever Happened to Baby Jane?* (1962), *The Flight of the Phoenix* (1965), and *The Dirty Dozen* (1967), meaning he could arrange backing to form his own studio and announce he would henceforth make movies under "The Associates and Aldrich" banner. He wanted to demonstrate to the industry that he could operate as a successful independent filmmaker away from the politics and control the major outfits exerted.

Speaking of *The Dirty Dozen*, a World War II story that was estimated by MGM to be their blockbuster movie for 1967, the studio decided that they'd hold a sneak preview in the 4200 seat Chicago Theatre.

Prior to the screening, Aldrich and I went to the projection room to meet the man who could make or destroy our cinematic event. Robert, with all the charm in the world, thrust half of a $50 bill into the projectionist's hand.

"If the film is kept in focus, the sound levels are maintained to my requirements, and there are no defects in the projection, then – and only then – you'll get the other half of the bill."

It is amazing how many times this trick ensured perfection in the many other screenings we attended!

Robert also insisted that any 35mm print that was to be used at a preview or premiere be run ahead of time to make sure that the reels were undamaged and in order. So many projectionists would say "sure, don't worry," but it does pay to worry. One such mishap occurred at an all-industry screening at the former Directors' Guild building in Hollywood.

On A Clear Day You Can See Forever (1970) starring Barbra Streisand was entering its fifth reel when the screen changed to Clint Eastwood in scenes from *Paint Your Wagon*. The producer, Howard Koch, apologized profusely to the star-filled audience, and everyone adjourned for drinks in the lobby while a frantic messenger was sent out to find the missing reel from Paramount Studios. Aldrich was determined that this would never happen to any of his films.

In 1968 I was dispatched to London for the start of filming on *The Killing of Sister George,* which Robert was directing. It's a curious story about how George (Beryl Reid) plays a cheerful district nurse in a BBC soap opera, but when her character is killed off she realizes that the only other job she can get is the voice of a cow in a children's tv program. Her life begins to fall apart, and adding further complication to matters, her lesbian lover, Childie (Susannah York), has an affair with a tv producer.

Lesbianism was a quite a taboo subject matter in the late '60s, and there was I being asked to set up a publicity campaign to promote it!

I arrived at my London hotel room only to hear the news that Bobby Kennedy had been killed. Being an ardent Democrat, Aldrich decided to go to the American Embassy in Grosvenor Square to sign the condolence book, and many of us followed suit. It wasn't quite the start to my campaign I'd anticipated, and there was a great air of disbelief and sadness throughout those first few days.

As expected, the film was very controversial and the newly formed ratings system of the Motion Picture Association of America immediately gave it an "X" rating. This meant that the *Los Angeles Times*' policy (shared by other quality print media) of not allowing any advertising for any film with such a rating, would prove disastrous for us at the box office. Aldrich sued, but after losing the first round with the MPAA and newspapers, realized that any appeals or further action would cost a personal fortune.

He relented and hoped word of mouth would get around and help the film's opening. In fact it did respectable business, and Beryl Reid won terrific reviews. It remains, in my opinion and indeed in many other people's, a much underrated story – and boy does it show Aldrich's diversity as a director when you think it was the first film he helmed following *The Dirty Dozen*.

Not long after our London sojourn, Robert embarked on his grandest movie in terms of crew, equipment and logistics – a World War II feature in the Philippines entitled *Too Late the Hero*. It was to star Michael Caine and Cliff Robertson, along with an assortment of British character actors. Aircraft were charted and we arrived in Manila only to discover that our location was miles and miles outside of the city, deep in the jungle. Another logistical problem – getting everything and everyone out there!

But then worse beset us. The Japanese actor, Ken Takakura, who was cast in a key role in the movie, was not allowed into the country because of the Philippine hatred of Japan stemming from World War II. It was quite unbelievable.

We had to re-jig things considerably, and filmed all of his scenes at the arboretum in downtown Los Angeles. And do you know something? No one could tell the difference!

During the filming, Aldrich and Cliff Robertson never saw eye to eye regarding the actor's approach to his role as the selfish Sam Lawson, and heated arguments would take place both on and off the set. As a result, Aldrich refused to change the production schedule to allow his nominated star to attend the Academy Awards that year. Robertson's Best Actor Oscar for his title role in *Charley* had to be presented at a later date, and he was denied his chance to climb to the stage and make his victor's speech.

Henry "Hank" Fonda was another star of the film, and he was a pleasure to work with and be with. We often chatted during breaks in filming, and with my having seen so many of his earlier films before I arrived in Hollywood, I was able to talk about specific scenes in some of them and ask about various co-stars, which I think pleasantly surprised him. Imagine my surprise when just before Christmas his wife Shirlee came to my office with a framed poster of one of his watercolors that he had personally signed. Within a year he was gone, but his legacy continues for ever more.

AMERICAN GRAFITTI
Feature film (1973)

American Graffiti was a small $750,000 feature written and directed by George Lucas, a young film maker who had just scored a success with *THX 1138*, which was a feature-length follow-up to a short film of (almost) the same name that he had made at university.

Lucas had his finger very much on the pulse and knew that a "coming of age" film centered on rock and roll, in 1962, would be a sure-fire

36 • *Jerry Pam*

hit. It was really about his life as he grew up, but in a style that was very different from what cinemagoers were used to, as it intercut four stories that didn't relate to each other. Consequently, the financiers didn't quite know what to do with it – they described it as a "musical montage with no characters and no story." It was very, very hard to get it off the ground, and on top of that it was a B movie. But Lucas persisted, and got the money.

Roll on to post-production, and a very good friend of mine, Ned Tanen, President of Universal Pictures, was having some problems with the film – which had by then been test-screened and received poor feedback.

Verna Fields, one of the finest film editors in the business, was brought in. She started by rearranging a few of the key scenes and completely changed the flow of the film, with the results being fantastic. Such was the esteem with which Verna was regarded, that she was later promoted to an executive role at Universal!

The backers now felt much more confident and were keen to mount a big publicity campaign around the film.

I persuaded them that radio was the medium we should concentrate on in the first instance. With a great selection of songs that would appeal to the record buying young folks, and a tie-in with a station to give away preview tickets – with hot dogs and soft drinks provided – we'd be sure of reaching our core audience.

The word of mouth was phenomenal, with disc jockeys all extolling the virtues of the characters in the film –as portrayed by Richard Dreyfuss, Harrison Ford, Ron Howard, and Kathleen Quinlan.

For the first press preview I decided to emulate the success of drive-in restaurants in LA, dressing the usherettes similar to waitresses and having them roller skate down the aisles, seating everyone. The media were delighted with their welcome – and gave us lots of valuable column inches! We then set up mass sneak previews across the country weeks in advance of the national release, further creating great word of mouth, plus it secured us more great air time for the soundtrack on local radio stations.

The film, produced by Francis Ford Coppola, became one of the biggest-grossing of the year, based on its meagre cost, and is in the AFI's top 100 films.

APOCALYPSE NOW
Feature film (1979)

There were many major problems with the shoot and locations in the Philippines (in fact there were problems before the shoot when the main lead was replaced by another actor, but that's an aside); and that coupled with Martin Sheen suffering a heart attack, and the director, Francis Ford Coppola, having marital problems, it all resulted in a major over-budget production.

My company hired a unit publicist to work with the crew in the Philippines, and as he was having a very tough time of it I realized that I ought to get involved out there too. United Artists, the backers and distributors, were getting very worried about all the rumors and gossip in the trade papers but, strangely, suggested I stay out of the fray. I could have probably limited some of the bad press they were getting, but the studio seemed to believe that they knew best how to handle things.

They favored an ostrich-style approach of burying their heads in the sand and waiting for it all to blow over, actually. Whatever I suggested fell on deaf ears, and so with my hands tied there was little I could do or contribute, and so I left the production.

The very same UA executives, by the way, backed *Heaven's Gate* shortly afterwards. Again, it went massively over-budget with many problems on location, not least a director who was given so much creative and financial freedom that he literally waited for grass to grow in fields he wanted to shoot in. The negative press proved very damaging to the studio's stock market listing and, in fact, brought the corporation to its knees and bankrupted them.

AVIATOR, THE
Feature film (2005)

This was the second time I was engaged to work with director Martin Scorsese on an Oscar campaign. It was a film about Howard Hughes, which Leonardo DiCaprio had nurtured for some years, and Michael Mann was originally lined up to direct. However, after completing the biopic *Ali*, Mann claimed he was physically exhausted and couldn't bear to think about directing another biopic so soon. That's when Scorsese was approached.

The film offered a fascinating insight into one of Hollywood's most enigmatic figures. There is always the danger in biopics that you try to tell

Memoirs of a Hollywood Publicist • 39

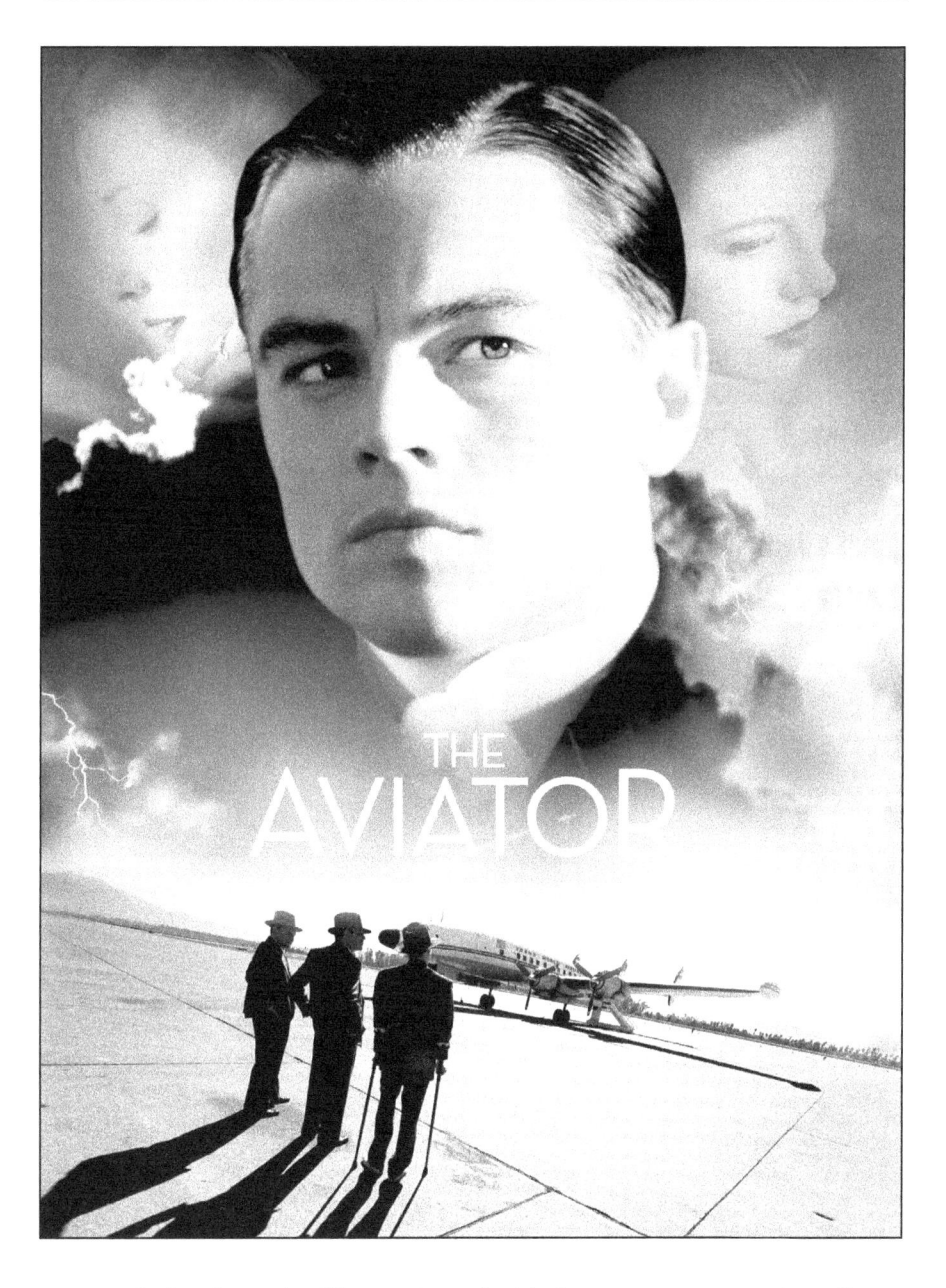

too much, but here the film-makers decided to concentrate primarily on Hughes' early film career, relationships, and his fascination with flight.

With terrific performances and critical praise, we knew we had a winner on our hands, but then came Clint Eastwood with *Million Dollar Baby*. The Oscar race really developed into a two-horse race between these two films, with the directors going head to head. Clint had won Best

Director for *Unforgiven*, whereas Marty had never received the trophy, despite many nominations.

Clint Eastwood is regarded as something of an icon in Hollywood, and having worked with him on the campaign for *Unforgiven*, I now found myself in the opposing camp preparing to go head-to-head with his campaign people.

One can theorize as to why any one film wins over another, but you just never know how academy members are going to vote. We went in with the most nominations, and Clint's film second to us, so we were the favorite. Indeed, on that night we won a clutch of Oscars, including one for Cate Blanchett's supporting actress portrayal of Katharine Hepburn. But Clint film's won bigger in the best actress, supporting actor, director, and film categories. Marty once again left without winning best director, but his day will come.

B

BAD DAY AT BLACK ROCK
Feature film (1955)

The screening of a final cut of MGM's soon-to-be-released drama was scheduled for studio chief Dore Schary and the publicity department to view at 10 o'clock one morning. We were in for a major surprise. The editor did not realize that Schary was totally without a sense of humor.

After the opening credits rolled, the first scene of the film introduced Spencer Tracy, portraying a one-armed man, alighting from a train in a western town. Immediately following this was the final scene of the movie, which showed Tracy boarding a train after solving his mysterious mission. The editor, Newell P. Kimlin, assembled these six minutes of footage of the two scenes and screened it thinking it was a great gag. He thought it was hilarious. It was! But, need I say, Schary didn't appreciate the joke. Newell received a tongue-lashing and the incident became the number one topic of conversation all over the studio. Schary was certainly a person to be feared.

BARBARIAN INVASIONS, THE
Feature film (2003)

This French-Canadian film was an unexpected hit. It concerns a dying man's regret of his past and how he brings old friends, family, and ex-lovers together to share his last hurrah.

His life is recreated by those around him, and appropriately there are no flashbacks, just reminiscences.

There was no doubt in my mind that it was a very strong contender for Best Foreign Film, so I set about my work. I handled the LA campaign, in which we had previews to include members from the medical profession who engaged in a Q&A on the ethics of euthanasia. It was a powerful debate.

Campaigns for foreign imports by the way, depend largely on Academy members viewing them in theatres and not on DVDs or videotape – and so I had to ensure I lured them to the screenings. The idea of the debate added significant interests to my RSVP list and thankfully, my efforts paid off and the film won the statuette.

BARRIE, GEORGE
Producer, Composer, Executive

It's always a bit daunting where you're an independent (in any field), wondering where the next pay check might come from, so you can imagine my great pleasure when, out of the blue, I received a call from Roger Moore, who was by now my good friend and client, suggesting I fly to New York to meet with George Barrie, the head of Faberge – the company famous for men's and women's toiletries. Moore was a director of the company and informed me that they were entering into movie production and would value my skills.

Meeting Barrie was unusual to say the least. At the appointed hour, I was taken by his secretary to a cavernous room that resembled a gigantic glass igloo. This served as his soundproof office. There, seated at the piano was the charismatic Barrie improvising a new song which he had just written, accompanied by one of his executives on the drums. This was the only time in my life that I was interviewed against the strains of a song which was to be Oscar nominated the following year!

A Touch of Class, as it happened, was destined to receive four nominations – for picture, best actor, screenplay and song ("All That Love Went to Waste") with lyrics by Sammy Cahn and that music by George Barrie. Actress Glenda Jackson won the first of her two Academy Awards too.

Brooklyn born Barrie's first venture in New York City was securing soda fountain concessions in half a dozen drugstores where he saw just what a thriving sector it was, and that's where he first thought about entering the cosmetic industry. He had taught himself to read music and play guitar, banjo, piano, clarinet, and saxophone; and whilst playing at an engagement in St. Paul he was introduced to a Minnesota cosmetics manufacturer, Raymond Lee, who having listened to the young man's aspirations

Memoirs of a Hollywood Publicist • 43

With George Barrie of Brut Films, and I seem to be looking very serious!

hired him to open a New York office for his Rayette line of professional products for beauty salons.

In a year Barrie was producing more business in the eastern states than the company was generating in the rest of the USA. Barrie eventually established his own company, Caryl Richards, which he named after his daughter and son. With grosses of over $7 million in l961 he bought out his former boss, Raymond Lee, and then two years later acquired Faberge.

Within ten years his annual gross had skyrocketed to $150 million and, in looking around for investment opportunities, Barrie decided that what he really wanted to do was produce movies.

There didn't seem to be any formal interview for hiring me, he just asked if I could design an advertisement for the trade papers, announcing the start of photography on his first motion picture, *Night Watch,* starring Elizabeth Taylor and Laurence Harvey.

Unfortunately, the film was delayed due to Harvey's ill health and, after several other disruptions, finally got underway. But once completed Harvey again fell ill and the release was further delayed. Tragically, Harvey died of stomach cancer shortly afterwards, aged just 45. The film was eventually released after the company's second production, the multi-award winning *A Touch of Class.*

Brut Productions (the movie arm of Faberge) was off to a great start. However, their early promise was relatively short-lived, as subsequent films never enjoyed the same success, though George Barrie received his second music nomination two years later with "Now That We're In Love" from *Whiffs.*

Joseph E. Levine, head of Embassy Pictures, was promised a "first look" screening of *A Touch of Class,* with a view to buying distribution rights. At the scheduled 8pm screening time, Levine arrived at the screening room and ordered his assistant to identify who was sitting in his favorite seat and have them move. As he did so, a booming voice shouted out,

"Who the fuck is Joe Levine and no, absolutely no, I will not move!"

I was standing next to Levine who turned to me and said, "What impertinence. I will stand for one reel of the movie and then leave."

Approximately 105 minutes later he walked down the aisle to see who indeed the loudmouth who wouldn't move was. It turned out to be Glenda Jackson. On recognizing her, he introduced himself saying, "Miss Jackson, this is one of the great performances I've seen in years. My name is Joe Levine, and fuck you too".

She rose from her seat and they embraced to the applause of everyone seated around her. Needless to say, Embassy released the film and made a fortune.

I feel I owe a great deal to George Barrie as he introduced me to the Cannes Film Festival in 1972. It was an adventure that was to inspire me to become a perpetual visitor to the annual ten day festival forever more.

We checked into the Gray d'Albion Hotel, which at that time stretched down from its reconstructed current location all the way to La Croisette, the main highway through the city. Having seen To *Catch a Thief*, starring Cary Grant and Grace Kelly, which showed a view from my hotel window overlooking the Mediterranean Sea, I relived those moments in the film by dining on the veranda and observing the yachts sailing past.

On a subsequent occasion, I travelled to Cannes with Glenda Jackson and Faye Dunaway amid a fanfare and hoopla to promote a film project that, alas, was never to see the light of day. It centred around the life of personality Victoria Woodhull, and her sister, Tennessee. When the former ran for the presidency in 1872, women had not even gained the right to vote; and consequently she did not receive one single vote. Later, she was involved in a sex scandal with a minister of the cloth, Rev. Beecher Stowe, and eventually became the business advisor to Commodore Cornelius Vanderbildt. It was a story that had all the ingredients of a great film. Maybe, one day ...

Sadly, in just four years the Brut bubble of success had burst and another independent movie company bit the dust.

BEATLES, THE
Musical sensations

Ten years had passed since I first met studio publicist Walter Shenson at my newspaper in Beverly Hills, when he very nearly got me fired. So when my secretary now said a Walter Shenson was calling from London and urgently needed to speak with me, I was intrigued.

He said he had quit Columbia Pictures and was now about to embark on a career as a film producer – albeit, as it happened, primarily low budget films. He needed a publicist to "keep his name alive in Hollywood," especially as he'd need to attract the attention of distributors in the hope of selling his films.

I asked the usual preliminary questions: What is the title? Who is starring? Somewhat to my astonishment he said that there was no title and the cast was unknown. How on earth was I to create any excitement when the press' maxim in Hollywood was "only names make news?"

Shenson explained he'd signed a new singing group called The Beatles. "Who are they?" I asked.

The following February, 1964, they appeared on the *Ed Sullivan* TV show, on CBS, and the the whole of America learnt just who they were!

I'd meanwhile never heard of them, and found myself starting a campaign for an untitled film with an unknown cast, coming from a B-movie producer and a relatively unknown director named Richard Lester, who had only made one other feature. It wasn't exactly going to be an easy sell, that's for sure!

The working title of *Beatles 1* was improved upon in the third week of filming, when Ringo Starr came into the group's shared dressing room late one evening and said it had been "a hard day's night." That was it! United Artists, the distributor, immediately registered the title and the result was history.

Noted Welsh writer Alun Owen

With the Fab Four aka The Beatles onocation for *Help!*

Victor Spinetti, Richard Lester, the Beatles – I'm talking to George Harrison.

was signed to pen the screenplay, which was essentially written as being a documentary in a day in the life of the group. He devised a concept of showing the foursome travelling in limousines to and from recording sessions, restaurants, and anywhere they decided to hang out. By accompanying them when he started writing the script, he was able to gather insights into their characters which made for very humorous and entertaining scenes, highlighting their true personalities.

Director Richard Lester had a keen ear for music, having played jazz piano, and really understood their particular brand of music. They nicknamed him their "conductor" and though the Beatles became bored and tired of repeating their lines for different takes, their respect and affinity for Lester was such that they maintained the highest professionalism anyone could have asked.

A Hard Day's Night was a great learning experience for me, and when news broke in 1980 of John Lennon's death, I reflected on some of the important things I learned from him. He possessed an inherent sense of what publicity was all about, and he had a great understanding for the rhythm of publicity – knowing exactly how light or heavy to touch the accelerator on humor, sincerity, and all the salient points we needed to get across.

Despite the group's enormous global success, John remained very firmly grounded. I noticed he had a sincere innocence of his clout, while another part of him knew or sensed how to use that clout adroitly. For example, one night on location he revealed that he was writing a second book "A Spaniard in the Works." I sat with Lennon and Derek Taylor, who was at that time their public relations representative, while Lennon said he hoped *someone* would publish this new work. Hoped? They'd be clamouring for it! Such was John's modesty.

The movie cost $500,000 and wasn't expected to be a great money earner, but United Artists was reasonably assured that they would make a decent return on the soundtrack alone. Consequently, and rather bizarrely, the decision was made to open the film without the Beatles being part of the publicity campaign. My task was really to create awareness of the film and music to the kids. The lack of the Beatles themselves proved a spur to my inventiveness, as I dreamt up stunts like "Who Can Wear the Best Beatle Wig?"

In spite of the fore-rumblings of Beatle mania crossing the Atlantic, the film proved a tough sell. A preview screening for the press and entertainment industry I organized at the Directors' Guild Theatre in Hollywood attracted only twelve people.

However, when the big six daily New York papers printed excellent reviews, a climate of mild interest circulated California. We had a certain satisfaction in knowing that the (formerly) disinterested LA journalists were now being dragged to the film by their children!

The film went on to gross $12 million in the US alone, and has earned half that amount again in video and DVD rentals. You could say it was a smash hit.

Much of the success is, of course, down to director Richard Lester. He was very astute in realizing the Beatles' limitations when it came to acting (he rated Harrison as the best of the four). As such he employed a quick cutting style, utilizing a hand camera which has since been copied by many next generation movie-makers, to keep the story moving and the viewer focused on it; rather than the performances.

Incidentally the scene in a train, where Lennon is holding a Coke bottle sniffing it with both nostrils, received a mild applause when it originally opened. There was no drug culture then, and so the connection wasn't established, but a generation later, viewers revelled in the significance of the sequence. Maybe they're reading too much into it?

Further success came when The Academy of Motion Picture Arts and Sciences announced Oscar nominations for Alun Owen's original screenplay and George Martin's music score.

Following the film's terrific opening on August 11, 1964, the Beatles appeared (for the first time) at the Hollywood Bowl on August 23. It was a night I will always remember, as I escorted my nine-year-old daughter Lesley to meet Paul McCartney back-stage and have her photograph taken with him.

The concert lasted about 30 minutes, and it was virtually impossible to hear them over the extremely loud screams and whistles of the fans. Many of them tried to get onstage, ploughing through the water fountains, and the ensuing pandemonium really did mean Beatlemania had reached America.

Producer Walter Shenson, who had signed a two-picture contract with The Beatles, decided to move straight into another film though, as budget restrictions meant *A Hard Day's Night* was shot in black and white, he was now determined to up the ante and make the second film in color, and happily Walter asked me to join the company once again.

Filming commenced on Paradise Island in the Bahamas (it's hard work being a publicist, I promise!), on February 22, 1965. At virtually the same time as Sean Connery was filming *Thunderball* at an adjoining location.

Now, with a budget three times that of their first film, The Beatles were ecstatic that director Lester was again helming the production, tentatively called *Eight Arms to Hold You*. The zany story involved a high priest (Leo McKern) attempting to recover a sacred ring which Ringo had in his possession – and he chased poor Ringo around the world.

Far from struggling to illicit press interest this time, I was absolutely inundated with requests from the worldwide media, all clambering for photos and interviews.

United Artists announced they didn't like the title – even though the title song had been written – and Shenson needed to come up with something else. It apparently sounded more like a horror film than a music filled comedy romp. The last thing any publicist needs to hear when awareness has already been created of a title, and promotional material distributed accordingly, is that it's all changed. Thankfully Richard Lester informed John Lennon of our predicament right away, and the next day Lennon came in with a new song entitled "Help!" – that's how quickly compositions were created – and after a publicity hiatus of a week, the alternative title was trumpeted to the world. The song became a Grammy winner too.

As I got to know the fab four, I began to appreciate just how talented and passionate they really were. Paul McCartney, for instance, often composed songs he knew would never be recorded, partly because they were so irreverent, but he had something to say with them. One that I recalled was "Let's Bring Back Old Winnie," a tongue-in-cheek reference to the great British Prime Minister Sir Winston Churchill.

George Harrison was always questioning me about movies and said that if he ever made a lot of money he would form a film company to make his own films. True to his word, in the 1970s Handmade Films came into being with George taking an active role as executive producer on such films as *The Life of Brian, The Meaning of Life, The Long Good Friday, Mona Lisa* and *Withnail & I*. One of his other features was *Shanghai Surprise,* starring Sean Penn and Madonna, and in it George played a cameo role as well as writing all of the songs. His writing had always been independent of Lennon and McCartney (who often shared writing credits), and I remain convinced he composed "Within You Without You" during the shooting of A *Hard Day's Night*.

During *A Hard Day's Night*, Ringo was always shopping for rings – of all sizes and shapes – and this inspired Charles Wood, one of the writers of *Help!* to come up with the storyline of the chase for Ringo's ring.

Around this time I met one of the world's greatest photographers, Henry Grossman. He was assigned to shoot The Beatles for the cover of *Life* magazine, and arrived at our Balmoral Island location. For three days he waited, and waited, and waited without using his Nikon camera once. I became frustrated when it seemed the stars were being uncooperative, and when Grossman announced he

Ringo loved me really!

was leaving the next day I rapidly attempted to resolve the situation with The Beatles. They told me that they had been starved of female companionship at the desolate location, and were not happy. Fearing that such a valuable publicity break would be lost, producer Shenson swung into action and got them their desired companionship. They then posed happily, and very cooperatively, and the *Life* magazine cover was saved.

As we had three weeks of filming in the Bahamas, it was decided to capitalize on this wonderful location by flying in the New York press. It was a terrific idea, as after all, what member of the press would turn down a trip to the Bahamas? We got some wonderful coverage in exchange.

In fact, I nearly got more than I'd personally bargained for as when Marion Means, of the Hearst Headline Service, returned to her home base in New York and called to say that The Beatles had written a song about me titled "What is a Jerry Pam?". Too bad it was never recorded – could have been a big hit!

One of the many other visitors to Nassau was ex-Queen Saroya, who had just separated from the Shah of Iran. She was desperate to meet the famed quartet and they were joking most of the time that she was the first REAL queen they had ever met. This was prior to their investiture on October 26 when Queen Elizabeth II bestowed their MBEs (Member of the Order of the British Empire) medals. Many British war heroes protested and sent letters to British newspapers saying that they were sending their gongs back as a protest that such personalities as pop stars should be honoured. The papers thankfully gave praise to the group who had been Britain's best export and the protest died a natural death in a matter of days.

Security had always been a concern for The Beatles. They were mobbed everywhere they went, and moving them from A to B was often a logistical nightmare. When you're on a film, time is always

Press conference time, and Robery Vaughn gets in on the act too.

At The Dodger Stadium. Getting in was easy, it was getting out that was the problem.

of the essence, and so these delays became an issue at times. I tried in vain to get their manager, Brian Epstein, to listen to my idea of having them travel separately. After all, nobody would expect to see a single Beatle, or for that matter, recognize him if he wore a baseball cap and sunglasses. Brian said, "I am spending hundreds of thousands of pounds and dollars protecting my investment and they travel as a group." So many of the headaches were in fact self-inflicted ones.

When the group was booked to perform at Dodger Stadium we had a strategy meeting about getting them in and, more importantly, out without the crowd mobbing them. The stage was to be set up on the pitcher's mound, and at the conclusion of the show a helicopter would descend and hoist them off – before the sell-out crowd would know what was happening.

A week before the concert – TRAGEDY!!! A helicopter from radio station KMPC carrying Capt. Max Shumaker, who was reporting on traffic conditions on the L.A. freeways, crashed just outside, you guessed it, Dodger Stadium.

Back to the drawing board. It was decided to keep the stage set up and erect a tent alongside to act as a dummy dressing room, with personnel carrying clothes in and out while The Beatles were performing their 29-minute show. Positioned inside was a Lincoln limousine, which would eventually transport the valuable merchandise to the center field gates, which when opened would allow The Beatles to speed off to their rented home.

Unfortunately, the driver, who was not accustomed to transporting rock stars, went to the wrong gate and before it could be opened 500 fans blocked his path! The driver had the sense to reverse and proceed to the players' dugout where the boys were escorted to safety inside. But the fans refused to be moved and stayed next to the car with the hopes of spotting their idols return to it.

Meanwhile, plan C swung into action. A Brinks armoured truck was hired and the boys were to be smuggled out into it through a side entrance. That was fine until the driver, having never driven anything other than boxes of cash and valuables, panicked and collided with a concrete wall. The boys were brought back inside pending a plan D. Three hours later The Beatles were on the road again, now in the back of an ambulance – which, finally, proved a great decoy.

Since they were virtually prisoners in their rented house, the studio provided the boys with all the latest movies and projection equipment (this was before video) and they unanimously selected *Cat Ballou* – in which Lee Marvin starred in an Academy Award winning comedy role. They told me that they thought it was mildly amusing, but they hated the constant laughter. I realised the studio had delivered a print with an experimental laugh track that was being tested for drive-ins. When I reported The Beatles' negative reaction to Columbia, the laughter tracks were removed from all other prints.

* * *

Security, as I've mentioned, was always an issue with The Beatles around their overenthusiastic fans. Four such teenage fans once even hired a helicopter to fly over pop stars' rented house hoping to see one of their idols. They were actually harmless enough, just a little misguided, and when I discovered they had saved up for six months to make the trip, I rewarded them with a pass to a press conference at Capitol Records. They were over the moon.

Arranging simple outings, or rather what we'd consider simple, took a lot of organizing and subterfuge. I remember them discussing how they really wanted to meet Elvis Presley while in LA; Brian Epstein invited his manager, Colonel Parker, over to the house to see if they could work out how and where a meeting could take place. Parker arrived with gifts – boxes of classic albums, all recorded by Elvis. He and Epstein talked for an hour without coming to any conclusion, before Paul finally used his persuasive charm saying, "In England he'd come to one or all of our houses. So, in America can't we go to his house?"

With no photography permitted, they travelled to Elvis' mansion and the humble lads were amused, to say the least, by his six cars in the driveway. The king of rock and roll came out to welcome The Beatles, well three of them, into the house. He asked where John Lennon was. Paul said, "He's parking the cars."

One of the servants arrived with a pot of English tea and some biscuits and they all adjourned to the music room, where Elvis put a nickel in his jukebox which, appropriately, played "A Hard Day's Night." Later, over steaks and french fries they discussed their mutual "enforced incarceration" from the public, and said how they often wished they could go back to being just ordinary people who could walk the streets without interference or being mobbed. Lennon suggested that he might have been happier had he stayed an electrician; just being able to go to a newsagent, pick up a newspaper and read it in Kensington Gardens in London was something he knew he would never be able to do again.

After savoring chocolate sundaes from Elvis' soda fountain (he made the gooiest they had ever seen) they retired to the games room to play the slot machines. What a day!

* * *

One of the joys of publicity is in creating merchandising ideas for clients – and it is often possible to retain a percentage if all goes well! With this in mind, I came up with an idea for Ringo Starr while we were shooting *Help!* in the Bahamas.

The foursome had established a merchandising company called SELTAEB and I had to fly to New York to discuss my possible business arrangement, whereby I would submit a proposal together with a marketing plan. At that time I was involved in publicizing a film in Europe and had arranged to meet the lawyers at 10am on a Wednesday morning.

I arrived at Copenhagen airport two hours before the scheduled departure of my PAN-AM flight, and was surprised that the gate assignment never showed on the departure monitor. Then, instead a "DELAYED, SEE AGENT" sign appeared. The crowd of passengers milled around while a well-dressed, non-uniformed, Pan American executive explained that the afternoon flight had been cancelled and the only other flight would leave at 6pm. Women and children would be given first priority, and for once in my life I questioned this edict – it wasn't the Titanic, was it? I knew that if I didn't get to New York in time, I wouldn't get a second chance to become a millionaire! Luck was on my side however, and I was offered a place on the 6pm flight. I arrived in New York in plenty of time for my meeting – which turned out to be a disaster!

They loved my idea of every schoolgirl being able to buy Ringo's ring in a multitude of colors, but what they failed to disclose to me were the lawsuits they had filed against their franchisees, who were all behind in their remittances re the jewellery tie-ups. No new deals were being negotiated until these remittances were banked. Reality kicked me in the face, and I knew too well that by the time this was all resolved, the film would have run its theatrical course, faded from people's memories, and my plan would be virtually worthless. Foiled again.

Who would have thought though, 37 years later Miramax would secure the reissue rights and I would once again be doing the publicity campaign? Along with restoring the prints, there was a state-of-the-art new soundtrack featuring the thirteen original songs, including "Can't Buy Me Love" and "I Should Have Known Better." Producer Walter Shenson and I had many discussions on a new approach for the December 1, 2000 launch, but sadly he was taken ill and laid to rest on October 22. He didn't quite live to see another generation discovering what he had created on film all those years earlier. The film grossed a respectable $1 million in the US, on its fairly limited release.

There was to be a third Beatles' motion picture by the way, to follow the success of the other two and a 20- page draft outline was submitted to United Artists, who became very enthusiastic about it. It was to be a Western, entitled *Showdown at Gower Gulch*, with a story revolving (no pun intended) around Paul and Ringo caught in a crooked poker game in 1860's Missouri. George, being the sheriff, was required to lock them up pending a jury trial. Lennon, playing a notorious bank robber, hearing of the incarceration of his old-time buddies, would ride into town and effect a jailbreak.

At first they too seemed excited about making another movie, but that initial enthusiasm would dampen when they discussed how bored they'd been on the long *Help!* shoot. They eventually nixed the idea and Shenson gave up the project.

* * *

In 2002 the music world was surprised, and somewhat shocked, by the news that Sir Paul McCartney (as he had become) was to do battle with John Lennon's widow, Yoko Ono, over song credits. I had been present when Linda Eastman, who was to become Paul's first wife had, in a loud voice, questioned why John had to get a co-credit on "Michele" and "Yesterday," both of which were Paul's creations.

With Paul's "Back in the US: Live 2002" album, which includes 19 songs written by the famous pair, the credits are reversed and Paul receives first billing to Lennon. The acrimonious war of words with Yoko had again become public, and Paul took the attitude that his name should appear first on songs for which he had been mainly responsible.

How the original order of credits had been determined is interesting. Their manager, Brian Epstein, had set a meeting for the two song smiths in his office one day, and because of Paul's late arrival the "crediting" decision was made. Subsequently, Epstein said that this would stand for the present and future. He would later evaluate the contributions by both and make any necessary changes – which he never did, of course. Now, years later, Yoko's attitude was that Paul benefited from John's "Strawberry Fields" which was his solo composition; so she has stood firm.

This brings me to the point of The Beatles break-up. From 1968 to 1971 there had been arguments, splits and rumours of reconciliation.

Paul eventually went to the High Court seeking a declaration that the business, under the name of "The Beatles and Co," constituted by a deed of partnership dated April 19, 1967 and made between the four Beatles, be dissolved. Prior to this move, Lennon had already announced that he would not work with the group again, as his recordings with Yoko and other interests were taking all his time. It was always Lennon's contention, which he voiced in the *Rolling Stone* magazine, that Paul tried to dominate the group and The Beatles were fed up being sidemen for him.

My contention is that drugs entered their lives, and with Lennon's admission to having taken pills during the filming of *A Hard Day's Night* and marijuana on their second film *Help!*, rational thinking went out the window. Plus there were the women in their lives; as the old saying goes "you cannot fight pillow talk," which I believe is nearer the real reason.

After the break-up, Paul went on to prove himself an extremely talented and accomplished musician, and carved out one of the most successful solo careers of any artist. So why, decades later, did he feel it necessary to reverse the song credits that had made him world famous? It puzzles me. What does it prove? What will it change?

I didn't meet George again until he created Handmade Films – in an attempt to revive the British film industry by producing smaller movies that would become the classics of tomorrow. My representing Michael Caine, the film's star, allowed me to visit the set of *Mona Lisa* and as executive producer, George was in attendance and paying attention to all aspects of the production. It was good to see him again, and share a few happy memories of the films we worked on. His death from cancer in 2001 created an avalanche of stories in the media, in which he was often referred to as the "Quiet Beatle" and underrated. He certainly was.

When ABC television produced a major special devoted to The Beatles several years ago, a big surprise in the show was Ringo Starr's added conversations of his experiences with the famed group. His witty stories and anecdotes about the way they all lived and performed revealed another side to his personality – a side I had not previously known. The camera on *A Hard Day's Night* loved him, and consequently he was immediately offered roles in Terry Southern's *Candy,* as the Mexican gardener, and in *The Magic Christian*. Though the films were not well received he was praised for his performances and has acted many times again since. His

George, John, Ringo and Paul. Four down to earth guys who I'm proud to have worked with.

marriage to Barbara Bach, with whom he starred in a bizarre film called *Caveman*, has lasted over 30 years; and his tours keep him in the limelight with fans around the world.

Individually and collectively, the fab four have brought much to the world. Their contribution to modern culture, music, and film should not be overlooked. I'm very pleased and proud to have known and worked with them at the height of their fame.

Oh, and had United Artists foreseen the group's ongoing fame and fortune, they probably wouldn't have agreed all rights to their films would revert to Walter Shenson after 15 years – which made him a multimillionaire! But hindsight is a wonderful thing, isn't it?

BERGMAN, INGRID
Actress

One of my childhood idols was Ingrid Bergman. Since first seeing *Casablanca*, I was captivated by her beauty and made a point of seeing every film in which she appeared.

She idolized her father – her sole living parent, who was an artist – but sadly when she turned 13 he passed away and she was orphaned. An uncle looked after her and encouraged her to follow her dreams of becoming an actress. She chose to attend the Swedish Royal Drama School after discovering Greta Garbo had attended years earlier. At the age of 17 she made her film debut, albeit in a bit part, in *Landskamp*. A few years later in 1935 came a much bigger part in *Munkbrogreven*. After several more films she starred in 1936's *Intermezzo* as Anita Hoffman. Luckily for her, movie mogul David O. Selznick saw it and sent a representative from MGM to secure the English rights to the story, and to sign the beautiful Miss Bergman to a contract. The remake of the film was a hit and so was Ingrid. Her beauty was unlike anything the movie industry had seen before, and her acting was superb.

Perhaps her most famous role came ten years after her first appearance on camera, when she starred opposite Humphrey Bogart in the aforementioned *Casablanca*. The wonderful *Gaslight* followed (for which she won Best Actress Oscar) and a few years later, following her performance in the title role of *Joan of Ark,* churches everywhere displayed her image. Their subsequent removal following her affair with Roberto Rossellini – whom she had fallen in love with on the set of *Stromboli* and left her husband (and daughter) for – caused her much distress. Hollywood was appalled by her actions, but she had no regrets of the years she spent with Rossellini; she even starred in five more of his films – which were, alas, all failures. She returned to English-speaking cinema in 1956, seven years after leaving her first husband, in *Anastasia* – for which she won her second Oscar. Her career bounced back.

Captivated by Ingrid Bergman.

Liv Ullmann was a great friend of Ingrid's (they starred together in *Autumn Sonata* in Sweden in 1978) and I'll forever remember the story Liv told me about a time they both went to see a movie. It began very slowly and gradually got worse as the plot tried to unfold. Ingrid turned to Liv and said "I am leaving. I don't like the film and I don't have time to waste watching rubbish."

"That was her philosophy for life" said Liv, "she was only happy when she could be doing something useful for herself and her friends. I really loved her for the woman, not the actress."

I was fortunate to work with Miss Bergman on *Murder on the Orient Express* and relished her great sense of humor. She told me how she roared with laughter when she saw the movie theater poster for a film she made with Warner Baxter and Susan Hayward – *Adam Had Four Sons* at 2:30, 4:30, 6:30 and 8:30pm. "He must have been some guy!" she exclaimed.

Her beauty captivated all who met her. I remember working on *The Secret of Santa Vittoria* with Anthony Quinn, and Ingrid's name was mentioned. He turned and said "I could not take my eyes off her, Jerry, when we were filming *The Visit*. She seemed to visually seduce everyone she came into contact with."

After working with her on the movie, I was delighted to learn that she was returning to the stage after some 18 years. With great triumph she opened at the LA Ahmanson theatre in *More Stately Mansions* with Colleen Dewhurst. I went backstage to congratulate her and she invited me to lunch the following week. We talked for hours, but before I left backstage that first night, I saw Alfred Hitchcock come over and he asked Ingrid "Did you get my card which said 'Best Wishes for a faulty stocking'?" She replied that she did, but didn't understand it. He laughingly exclaimed "A long run!"

A few years later in 1982, my friend Jean Negulesco called me with the sad news that Ingrid had died of cancer. He related a very touching story about her last role in a TV movie *A Woman Called Golda*, in which she played the title role of Israeli Prime Minister Golda Meier. On the final day of filming Ingrid went through seven takes on what was a very simple scene and the director queried her if all was well. After all, she had acted her way through four weeks of intensive shooting, with barely a second take of any scene being needed. She replied, "This is the last time I will ever appear in front of the camera and I did NOT want it to end."

She knew that she only had weeks left before her final departure.

A posthumous Emmy was awarded to her for her role as Golda Meir.

[see also **MURDER ON THE ORIENT EXPRESS**]

BALSAM, MARTIN
Actor

Martin Balsam was a stocky character actor who had made a bit of a name for himself during the early days of television drama – appearing in numerous live shows such as *Playhouse 90, Studio One*, and *Climax*. Naturally, a big-screen career soon followed and he became well known for roles in such features as *All the President's Men, Murder on the Orient Express*, and *Twelve Angry Men*.

I was assigned by United Artists to assist in a film of his that was experiencing problems in post production. I should point out I very rarely come in to a project at this point, as my main role is in handling press matters during production and pre-release. *A Thousand Clowns* was based on the hit Broadway show and director Fred Coe was in the editing suite and said it just wasn't coming together.

It isn't for me to speculate whether it was the director's or actors' fault, but the studio thought it was going to be a disaster and were desperate to salvage anything they could. I've publicized some great movies, and even a few mediocre ones, but I've never tried with one which even the director though was a turkey!

Thankfully a very talented editor named Ralph Rosenblum was drafted in to review the material, and with skilful and careful cutting, the film was crafted into one which many raved about as "the best film ever!" Wow.

In fact, all the critics raved and the film, supporting actor, writing, and music were all nominated, though, criminally, nowhere was the editing mentioned – which was the most vital part of this movie. As a publicist, I could hardly mount a campaign saying "without this editor the film stunk," though I must admit, I was disappointed that he was totally overlooked.

Of all the nominations, Martin Balsam was the only winner from the film. He was an interesting character.

Actors have been known to have short memories in real life, even though they have a marvellous capacity to remember their lines on movie sets. The day the nominations were due to be announced I had breakfast with Balsam at Nate 'N Als, a well-known deli in Beverly Hills. He said if he won the Oscar he'd like to hire me as his personal press agent.

You can probably guess the rest of the story – he won and that was the last I ever heard from him. No acknowledgment and no forwarding address to his New York home that's for sure!

I've been made similar promises in the past though when the actors in question fail in their bid for a nomination or Academy Award, they of course feel that as the mission was not accomplished, they couldn't afford to keep me on (or words to that effect). Meanwhile, here was an example of a winner. C'est la vie.

BAUM, MARTIN
Hollywood agent

Martin (Marty) Baum was one of Hollywood's legendary characters, and as head of the Creative Artists Agency represented pretty much a who's who of Hollywood A-list talent. He actually once sold an actor client to producer-director Stanley Kramer for the comedy *It's a Mad, Mad, Mad, Mad World* only to discover that the thespian had died six months before!

He was also director Robert Aldrich's agent for years. They had a love-hate relationship and almost came to blows when Baum left the agency to become head of ABC Films. Aldrich had a project of a Ted Flicker script, *The Crowded Bed,* with Woody Allen, Goldie Hawn, and Joe Namath set to star, and Baum, prior to becoming the studio executive, had sold this very package to ABC Films. However, on assuming his new role at the company he rejected the project.

Aldrich, in his fury, accused Baum of disloyalty. Understandably so; particularly as he had been instrumental in getting the agent his new job. Baum retaliated by saying "I often had to sell crap as an agent but now as an executive I don't have to eat it."

The feud lasted several years though when Baum resumed his role as an agent, having left ABC, Aldrich re-signed with him!

BEATTY, WARREN
Actor, Director, Producer

Warren Beatty is an enigma – brilliant, but he was always very suspicious of everyone and everything. You ask him a question and he asks you six questions back about your one. Trying to analyze the psychology of the man is impossible. Years of being a star, a superstar, and having tremendous fame obviously plays a big part in that. Though as annoying as he could be in this respect, he is one of the most charming men you could hope to meet.

I worked with him on several movies and was always amazed at his ability to extract whatever information or service he needed, by pure charm – I do not believe there is another actor in Hollywood who can make one feel so appreciated. There is nothing phony in his attitude and I really believe he is interested in everything and everybody. But, as I say, he is deeply suspicious!

An example comes to mind. After filming wrapped on *Reds* in 1981, a reporter from *Pravda* came to see me, using the pretext of wanting to publicize the film to get an interview with Warren for his Moscow newspaper. Immediately Warren turned my request into 20 questions: Who was it?; Why was he being sought?; What would they ask?; Did the interviewer think he had pro-communist sympathies, etc? Needless to say the meeting never took place.

Warren Beatty as Dick Tracy.

Reds, which I considered Warren's masterpiece, was honored by the Academy with Oscar nominations for director, producer, writer, and lead actor – all Warren Beatty! I really believe he lost out to *Chariots of Fire* with the Best Picture award due to the British film's stirring soundtrack – which carried it with great fanfares of publicity for a long period of time.

One of the main criticisms of *Reds*, from Academy members, concerned lack of identification of the interviewers who were sidebars of the film. Warren, for some inane reason was against revealing their identities. Paramount, the film's distributor, subsequently had standees placed in theater lobbies to remedy the situation. I guess it was a compromise of sorts?

Warren's philosophy is that he should have a completely "hands on" approach; and he does. He stands his ground too. For instance, he refused to edit *Reds* for TV – conforming to the station's edict that the 11pm evening news could not be delayed. It was delayed for him!

I learned much from Warren during the other movies I worked with him on; *Shampoo, Bugsy, Heaven Can Wait*, and *Dick Tracy*. He's a very talented all-rounder and salesman.

BOGART, HUMPHREY
Actor

Was he more famous in death than in life? A legend in our time, Humphrey Bogart, or Bogie as he was known, may have quite possibly been Hollywood's most charismatic and enduring star. His death in 1957 robbed the movie-going public of an actor whose portrayal of off-beat characters is nowhere to be seen today.

My only meeting with Bogie was unusual to say the least, and it gave me some insight into, and odd facts about, his most popular film, *Casablanca*.

Generally, I have always been a poor sailor – becoming seasick at the drop of a hat. Friends, who sail or fish on weekends, have invited me on numerous occasions to join them for a day on the briny, and I've always made excuses to avoid the mal de mer.

However, in what I can only describe as a moment of madness, I accepted one friend's request to sail to Catalina Island, just off the California coast, in his new forty-foot yacht. It was supposed to be an honor to be on an inaugural voyage, and as it was on a summer weekend I felt that the sea would be calm with gentle breezes. Was I in for a surprise!

We left Long Beach harbor at 10pm. At 2am I realized that we had to be lost. Without boring you with details of the zigzag course we made during the night, our vessel docked at Catalina harbor at about 5:30am on the Sunday morning. We were tired and hungry. As we disembarked, a voice shouted to the four of us from a schooner alongside which rejoiced in the name of SANTANA.

"What the hell are you guys doing so early on a Sunday morning?" Bellowed what seemed to be an old-time sea captain, standing on deck with a coffee mug in one hand and a cigarette in the other.

Humphrey Bogart aboard his boat.

"Fancy some hot coffee with a little something inside?" he enquired.

Through our bleary eyes, we realized it was a smiling Bogie in front of us, in a seafaring outfit, shouting to us to come aboard and join his group of friends – who had obviously spent the night celebrating.

What a thrill! My joy of meeting one of my screen idols knew no bounds. I am sure the coffee was laced with rum – but it felt so good after our arduous journey.

Small talk developed and Bogie told me that he had great misgivings on accepting his role in *Casablanca*, as there wasn't a completed script. Accept it he did though, and what a good judgment that was.

I discovered that Dooley Wilson, in the pivotal role of Sam, the piano player, could NOT play the keyboard and they had to enlist the services of Elliot Carpenter, a staff musician, who played on the sidelines while Dooley fingered as best he could. The magic of movies, eh? Though Jack Warner, head of the studio that bears his name, hated that haunting melody "As Time Goes By" and ordered the film's producer Hal Wallis to remove it. When it was discovered that this would cost $50,000, a fortune in 1941, the directive was withdrawn.

Bogart also told me that during World War II, and in particular in l943, all U.S. mail from the Middle East was censored if there was any mention of his name – as this would indicate that the servicemen were either in or near the African port of Casablanca.

I never realized that I would eventually be involved with *Casablanca*, albeit on its reissue, many years later. United Artists Corporation acquired the distribution rights to the movie, and I was assigned to handle the publicity of the newly restored print. The premiere was held in Beverly Hills at the Doheny Plaza Theatre, which is now known as the Writers' Guild Theatre.

The great Edward G. Robinson in *Little Caesar*, also restored, accompanied the *Casablanca* re-release, and new prints were made for the occasion. Hollywood celebrities turned out in force for the unique presentation.

My first task was to convince the only living star from the movie, Paul Henreid (who played Victor Laszlo), that his presence at this all-star event was vital. He'd become a TV director following the decline in leading man roles in the late 1950's. At first he seemed unwilling to participate, unless my publicity release stated that he relinquished his first position billing above the title at the personal request of Jack Warner. At that time Henreid was the number one star at Warner Bros. and Bogart was on the way up, but not yet there. But, all these years later Bogart was of course the name everyone knew – he was the star. I couldn't even try and take that away, so I had to convince Henreid that, as far as this premiere was concerned, he would be in first position for the entire promotion, and he agreed to come (phew) — so long as we provided transportation.

Elliot Carpenter would be an added bonus, I thought, but finding him was no easy task. He was not listed in any telephone books in Los Angeles, nor was he still working at any studio or production company, but via the Motion Picture Industry Health and Pension Plan I tracked him to a house in the Echo Park district of Los Angeles. He didn't have a phone, so an uninvited visit seemed my only way in.

The outside of his wooden house appeared to be on its last legs, so I approached with caution and knocked on the battered door, which was hanging on rusty hinges. After an age, a kindly old African-American greeted me on the door step as if I was a long-lost cousin. Two coffees later the 86-year-old, who could not stop reminiscing about his Hollywood career, finally drew a breath – and I got in with my proposition. "Would you play, during the cocktail hour, songs from the movie? You would receive $1,000 for your services."

He looked surprised.

"For that fee I would play all night".

And so it was. "As Time Goes By" and "It Had to Be You" echoed through the lobby. Henreid and Carpenter were applauded by the throngs who congregated near the vintage upright piano.

Julius Epstein, one of the Oscar-winning writers, came along too and added some of his experiences. Dooley Wilson, he said, was really a drummer, not a pianist, and the Claude Rains character was modelled after a con artist he once met in Las Vegas! Ironically, Dooley was offered a gigantic contract to take a cross country tour of America, playing the piano selections from the film. Alas, he knew that he couldn't fake this in live performances and declined.

Tears of joy and sentimentality made the evening one to be long remembered. Elliot Carpenter was sent home in a chauffeured limousine, wiping away his own tears as he left.

A while later, at the San Francisco Film Festival, I was treated to a dinner in the wine cellar of the old "Ernies" restaurant. It was a party following the festival's opening night gala and I was seated next to the great director Joseph Mankiewicz, who started a vigorous conversation with "What's your favourite film?" After such epics as *Ben-Hur*, *Gone With the Wind*, and *Citizen Kane* were discussed, I piped up with *Casablanca*. Mankiewicz started to tear the film apart.

"There was no such thing as a 'letter of transit' and therefore the climax of the movie was false," he opined.

I rose to the defence.

"To the movie-going public, seeking escapist entertainment, belief can often be suspended. After seeing a great love story unfold, set against a dramatic background, does one really care if a 'letter of transit' actually exists? It's only a movie."

After a little applause, the conversation turned to other topics.

On August 19, 2002, the Academy of Motion Picture Arts and Sciences presented *Casablanca* as part of its series of weekly screenings of all the Oscar winning movies. This was to tie in with the Academy's 75th anniversary celebration. I was again able to re-live this near perfect motion picture on the big screen without worrying about the facts or fiction. I simply love it as a movie!

[see also **HUSTON, JOHN**]

BOYD, STEPHEN
Actor

On the set of *Ben-Hur* in Rome, *The Hollywood Reporter*'s Army Archerd covered the famed chariot race for fun with his 8mm movie camera. On returning to Los Angeles he found himself speaking with some executives

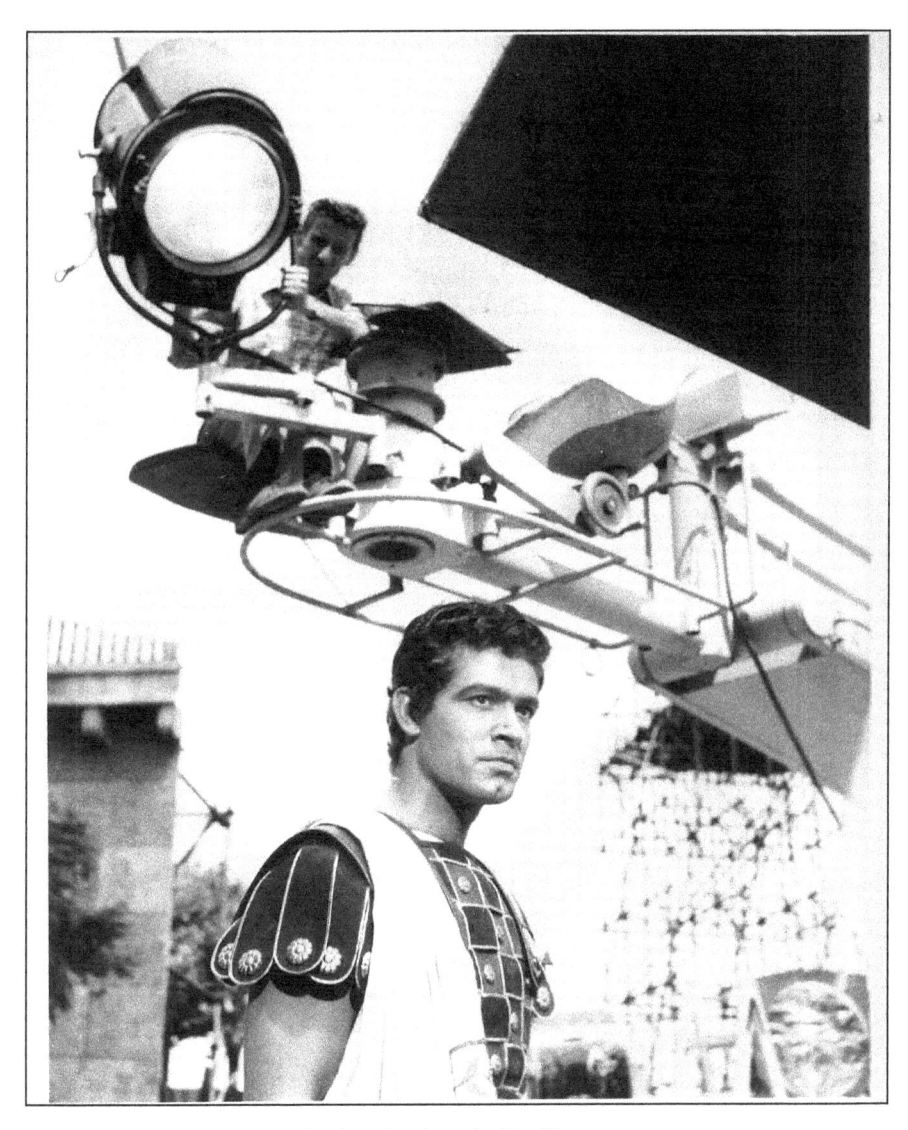

Stephen Boyd on the *Ben Hur* set.

at MGM, who had not received film of the race back from Rome at that time, so he went along and showed them his footage. That earned him a lot of brownie points.

Army told me he felt Boyd would be a major star and that I ought to contact him. It was favor returned for the many stories I'd given Army over the years.

At the LA premiere I introduced myself to Boyd and half expected to be rebuffed. How wrong I was. He suggested we have coffee the following week. He explained he was already signed to a large publicity office (Rogers and Cowan) but after hearing my pitch he promised to keep me in mind for the future.

Months went by and when at a party hosted by my actor friend Michael Callan, I bumped into Stephen Boyd.

"I was going to call you in about four weeks in the hope that you were still as enthusiastic as when we first met, so we could discuss my future. I'm coming to the end of my contract," he said.

I certainly was still as enthusiastic! I duly became his publicist and confidant, and for the next 17 years we travelled the world together, enjoyed each other's company on the tennis courts and in restaurants far and wide.

With my friend Stephen Boyd.

Towards the end of our working relationship I unfortunately witnessed his fall from grace in Hollywood, which seemed to follow his conversion to Scientology. It wasn't a subject we discussed in any great depth, but his beliefs – sometimes expressed very vocally in public – caused concern amongst the studio executives, and they decided he was no longer bankable nor should he be the face of their output.

But I look back on the fun times we shared; one was quite hair-raising, in Cairo, where he was starring in John Huston's *The Bible*. Boyd arranged a meeting with the number one movie star in Egypt – Fatem Hamama – who, despite being separated, was technically still the wife of Omar Sharif. She wanted to take us to an event unique to the Middle East, and after driving in her tiny car to Old Cairo we arrived at a hall where more than one hundred Whirling Dervishes were dancing in what seemed to be a trance. This continued for ages and was quite spellbinding to watch. Then, our hostess was spotted by many of the onlookers who started to make their way over to her, so we decided to make good on our escape.

However, a crowd of more than 30 Egyptians immediately surrounded our car and began knocking on the window, and then started rocking it back and forth in what I guess they saw an attempt to get the famed movie star to open her window. I was really quite scared as they were a pretty mean looking lot. Luckily the police arrived and we hastily drove back to her apartment, which I remember overlooked the Pyramids of Giza, and finally relaxed while her cook rustled up a late supper. Stephen laughed about the earlier events of the day, but I told him his idea of a fun time was not necessarily one I shared.

One of Stephen's proudest moments was when he became an American citizen in 1964. I hosted a party at my house to celebrate his naturalization, and his *Ben-Hur* chariot competitor Charlton Heston was on hand to offer congratulations, along with Clark Gable's widow, Kay, Cesare Danova (the first choice for *Ben-Hur*, but this casting vetoed as he was an unknown), Esther Williams, Fernando Lamas, Elke Sommer, and Bob and Rosemarie Stack.

Another happy memory of working with Stephen was when a friend, producer Euan Lloyd, invited me out to Almeria, in southern Spain, for *Shalako*, which starred Sean Connery, Brigitte Bardot, and Stephen Boyd. It was an 1880's western embracing European aristocratic game hunters in New Mexico being ambushed by Apache Indians. Almeria was the flavor of the month for westerns, both American and European, due to the rugged terrain and the great weather. Rival movies were being shot at the same location unbeknownst to us, and in one moment, as the rival company's herd of horses thundered towards us, it looked as though we were in the famous Battle of Bunker Hill at the turn of the last Century!

At the Aguadulce Hotel, where we were all staying, there was a suite which Brigitte Bardot had occupied, and following her departure a sign was put up which stated "BRIGITTE BARDOT SLEPT HERE." One of the crew pencilled underneath "With Whom?"

I could have answered this query but was pledged to silence by all concerned!

Sadly, the finished film lacked pace and energy and seemed to move very slowly under (McCarthy blacklisted) Edward Dmytryk's direction, and certainly never contained the excitement that the script engendered.

Stephen Boyd died on June 2 1977 of a massive heart attack. He was on a golf course in the San Fernando Valley.

BRAZIL
Feature film (1985)

Without a doubt, this was one of my strangest ever assignments, in so much as I was asked to publicize a movie that was never going to be released – or rather, be seen.

Directed by Terry Gilliam (of *Monty Python* fame), the Universal Studios' picture launch date was continually delayed because of the subject matter – the studio felt the public wouldn't understand it! Quite why they green-lit it in the first place is not for me to ask. They'd spent millions on it and now had this "dystopian science fiction film" just sitting on the shelf.

I think I was engaged as part of the studio's attempts to show they were doing something, though I didn't have a release date or a publicity budget.

The exasperated Gilliam eventually took out trade press advertisements asking "Please Mr Sheinberg, when are you going to release my picture *Brazil*?"

The two-hour twenty-minute film was eventually released, though with very little advertising or promotion – and I'm still not sure I understand it to this day.

BRANDO, MARLON
Actor

[see **LAST TANGO IN PARIS**]

BURTON, RICHARD
Actor

One of my closest friends in Hollywood was Valerie Douglas. A phenomenal lady and Richard Burton's long term manager. In the late 1970s, Valerie felt the once shining star of the great actor was somewhat diminished. Far from regaling his acting achievements, gossip magazines were then just full of stories about his life with Elizabeth Taylor, his excessive drinking, and lavish lifestyle aboard their yacht, Kalizma.

My association with him really started following his second marriage and divorce from Elizabeth Taylor in 1976. He said of her: "I might run from her for a thousand years and she is still my baby child. Our love is so furious that we burn each other out."

I was asked to divert publicity from his private life and towards his career. He was soon to start a new film called *The Wild Geese*, with Roger

Richard Burton in *The Wild Geese* with Richard Harris, Roger Moore and Hardy Kruger.

Moore and Richard Harris. Happily, I was representing the film's producer Euan Lloyd at that time too.

At Burton's rented Beverly Hills mansion we discussed a campaign strategy. I have to admit I was in awe of him; he had such a powerful, commanding presence. He certainly enjoyed being a major star too, and that manifested itself in him always expecting the best seats on a plane, always getting a table at the top restaurants, getting tickets for sold-out theater shows and so on; he never believed a miner's son could become a legend. I guess one had to have a giant ego to become so famous?

He asked me if I had any regrets in life. I said very few. He went on, "I regretted all cocktail parties. I would have far rather have been with the crew, who were my friends, in a pub somewhere telling funny stories." It revealed a more humble side to him that I'd previously not seen. He continued, "Do you know at one time I was drinking nearly three bottles of vodka a day?" I said I didn't know that, and he then said – rather taking me aback – "but my one big regret Jerry, was the inability to have a son."

I was in awe of the man one minute, annoyed by his star pretensions the next, but then totally melted by his humility and sincerity.

Burton told me that he was the twelfth of thirteen children and realized his only way out of an impoverished Welsh childhood was by acquiring knowledge from books – and so he read avidly. From there he developed his passion for the arts; in fact, his command and understanding of English poetry led him to teach for a term at Oxford University in the early 1970s. He was quite an intellectual. He travelled everywhere with what he called his "book bag." It included a complete set of Shakespeare, a Bible, and a dictionary of English slang.

Acting as Burton's chauffeur on the publicity trail allowed me to glimpse many fascinating insights into his life and career. I also realized that, together with Peter O'Toole (although O'Toole was later awarded an honorary Oscar), he holds the record for the most Best Actor Oscar nominations (7) without a single win. A great tragedy. There are so many stories and anecdotes I remember, and a few I should probably forget.

One of my favorite stories was concerning the opening night of his *Hamlet* at London's Old Vic Theatre. A hysterical backstage manager informed Burton that "the great man will be sitting in the front row tonight." Burton stepped on stage to see the imposing figure of Winston Churchill. After several minutes, Burton realized that Churchill was mouthing his lines, and so he sped up and slowed down – Churchill did likewise. At the end of Act One, Churchill disappeared from his seat and there was a knock on Burton's dressing room door.

"My Lord Hamlet, may I use your lavatory?" asked Churchill.

Interestingly, Burton went on to play Winston Churchill in the 1974 tv movie *The Gathering Storm*. He is one of the few, if not the only, actors who have played that part who can say he shared a toilet with the great Prime Minister!

Another couple of fun stories were about the epic production of *Cleopatra*. After filming was abandoned in London due to many problems with the weather and Elizabeth Taylor's ill health, Stephen Boyd left the film. The studio was keen to cast Richard Burton in his place, as Mark Antony, and willingly paid the stage production of *Camelot* $50,000 to secure his release; that was in addition to his reported $75,000 fee for the film itself. Liz Taylor received a million dollars.

Burton said he felt terribly uncomfortable in the first love scenes, and it wasn't until director Joe Mankiewicz showed him the rushes that he said, "they look so believable." In fact, true to their real and reel life.

In one of the movie's key scenes, thousands of spectators and soldiers on horseback hail their queen as she arrives in Rome. Burton said it was quite probably one of the hottest days of the year, and after many hours of setting it up, the director finally called action, only to scream "Cut!" a minute later. In the center of a massive square, into which Cleopatra was to enter, there was a very determined Italian ice cream vendor attempting to sell his wares to the captive crowd of extras!

Burton was quite a serious and intense man at times too, particularly when he spoke of his relationships. He told me, quite spontaneously, that his feelings of guilt at having left his first wife Sybil never went away. He reassured everyone (himself included) by saying "I gave her everything I had in the divorce settlement, which was enough to last her forever."

Liz Taylor and he undoubtedly loved each other greatly, perhaps too much to be able to live together? He told me that much of his screen presence was attributable to her. "She made me a better actor" he said, and explained "one looks so different on a 30-foot-high movie screen, than one does on a stage. It made me conscious of every movement and gesture and how I carried myself on screen."

In 1976 he married Susan Hunt, and I must admit that I found her to be a terrific ally. Whenever I needed to ask anything media related I discovered if I put it to Susan first I'd invariably get a favorable response from

Me with Mrs Richard Burton, Elizabeth Taylor.

Burton, though he was quite often incommunicado due to his imbibing and, sadly, that illness – and it was an illness – ultimately resulted in his fourth marriage failure.

He was a tremendously wealthy man towards the end of his life and lived in Swiss tax-exile. Aaron Frosch, who was his financial advisor for most of his career, told me how Burton had made his life so complicated with a great number of staff and other people on his payroll – most of whom were unnecessary.

"At one time they numbered 35" said Frosch, "and while he and Liz Taylor became the first movie couple to command a million a movie, the money flowed out like a tidal wave and I could do nothing to stop it."

But Burton just enjoyed life. If money enabled him to be extravagant, then he was.

One year after divorcing Susan in 1982, he married Sally Hay. I never really got to know her, but mutual associates and friends said she was a terrific and calming influence on the actor. Sadly, the marriage only lasted a couple of years, as he died aged just 59.

That morning, I received a telephone call from producer Euan Lloyd. He was within days of starting shooting on *The Wild Geese II*, in which Richard Burton was to reprise his role of Allen Faulkner from the original.

"Jerry, I have just lost my leading man," said Euan.

I remember a cold chill ran down my spine. I couldn't quite believe the news. He seemed invincible.

It was a privilege getting to know the man behind the performance.

C

CAINE, SIR MICHAEL
Actor.

It was at a party hosted by Michael Callan in LA, in 1965, to celebrate the actor's role in *Cat Ballou*, where I first met Michael Caine. We talked about being fellow Londoners, and at the end of the evening he invited me to the set of his first Hollywood movie, *Gambit*, which was shooting at Universal Studios. That marked the beginning of our friendship, and when Michael began making more films in America I was delighted to be the first publicist he'd ever engaged.

Like many Brits at that time, he thought being represented by a press agent was inviting intrusion into his life. In fact, my job is more about controlling any intrusions and making life easier.

Our working association really commenced during the shooting of the World War II drama *Too Late the Hero*, in the Philippines in 1969, with Robert Aldrich directing. At the after-shoot luncheon, Michael mentioned the school he attended in London; I'd attended that very same school during World War II, though we never met. I was then immediately welcomed as a member of the Caine family, and we remain very close to this day. In fact, he was my best man at my second wedding in 1976 – and threw a fabulous reception for us at the Churchill Hotel in London.

Michael always insisted I be his guest in his Grosvenor Square bachelor flat in London whenever I was in town or just passing through en route to a location somewhere. I often met many of his friends there, and perhaps the most memorable of visitors was the late Peter Sellers, who arrived at 2:30 one morning following a well publicized liaison with a prominent member of the Royal Family at Buckingham Palace!

Saturday lunchtimes in London, when not working, were always spent at the Aretusa restaurant in King's Road Chelsea. Many actor friends often joined him: Roger Moore, Albert Finney, Denholm Elliott,

The Caine's wedding ceremony in Vegas. Dennis Sellinger is on the left..

Ronald Fraser, Larry Gelbart, and Leslie Bricusse being amongst them. Sunday mornings were always reserved for the weekly baseball game in Hyde Park, with the American contingent who were working and living in London, trying to teach their British counterparts the finer points of the game. Director Mel Frank, one such participant, used this little bit of "Americana" at the start of his film *A Touch of Class*.

One morning, in January 1973 at 8am, Michael called and asked me to organize his wedding to Shakira in Las Vegas that same night with no fanfare, no publicity, and being as secretive as possible.

We booked a flight, and upon arriving at the airport in Vegas took a taxi to the city hall, where I had pre-arranged a wedding license. There we met Michael's agent, Dennis Selinger, who had just flown in from London, to make up our foursome.

We drove along the famed Strip looking for one of the over-publicized wedding chapels for the nuptials. The one we chose just happened to be opposite the New Frontier Hotel – where we'd decided to hold our own little reception, and subsequently attended the dinner show which starred Keeley Smith and Louis Prima.

Realizing that we should have some photos of the wedding, I called an old friend – the United Press photographer in Vegas – who obtained a world exclusive in exchange for copies of the wedding photos.

We then boarded a late plane back to LA and the next morning Michael called me and said, "It seemed like only yesterday we eloped!"

Subsequently *Time* magazine called Michael and asked him where he would be honeymooning. He responded, as Shakira was pregnant, that they'd already had their honeymoon!

* * *

One of the great thrills of visiting Michael on film sets was in meeting his many co-stars. On a visit to England, when Michael was shooting *Sleuth*, I was privileged to have lunch with Laurence Olivier – who insisted that all of us call him Larry, and not Sir or Lord. This was the film that raised Michael to new heights as he went head to head in this wonderful two-hander with the great legend of the British theatre, and both were nominated for the Best Actor Oscar.

I used to telephone Michael from Hollywood at 10am (6pm in England) to discuss the various happenings on the movie scene, and to keep myself updated on any offers he'd received for future productions. During one such call he announced with great enthusiasm that he'd been sent a wonderful script and was going to have his agent negotiate. He told me about the story, the director, and the title – I couldn't help but laugh – I'd actually seen the script a week before!

When the script reached Michael's Hollywood agent and he read and considered it, it was then forwarded to his counterpart in London, who in turn read it and discussed its merits; meanwhile time passes rapidly. Then it was sent to Michael, who may or may not have been available to read it quickly, so the film's producer reckoned there is no interest and sent it to another actor – via me!

With that established process in mind, producer Irwin Allen called me one day saying he was looking for a star for the lead role in a movie that was scheduled to start shooting in two weeks. He needed a pretty immediate answer – within 24 hours – and I asked Michael if he was interested. Of course he was, but not without reading the script.

I told Michael that the screenplay would be on the 1pm TWA flight to London. It was to arrive at 7:30 the following morning and then be sent by courier to his house. He had to call me with an answer two hours later.

Thus, for better or worse, he starred in his first Hollywood disaster movie *The Swarm* with Henry Fonda, Olivia De Havilland, Richard Widmark, Richard Chamberlain, Fred MacMurray, Katherine Ross, Lee Grant, and Jose Ferrer.

With the tightening grip of the British tax regime, when the rate hit 96% for high earners, many actors left the UK. On the back of *The* Swarm, Michael could afford to buy a big house in America, and in fact stayed for eight most rewarding years. Though quite a few of the movies he subsequently made were away from Hollywood, they were initiated there.

Michael and Shakira seemed to enjoy life in LA. They were the life and soul of many parties – either hosted by them or at friends' lavish homes. It was considered a coup if the Caines attended.

Soon a group of mates began gathering every Sunday at the Caine house for brunch. Aside from being a wonderful host, Michael also displayed his talent for serving up a delicious roast leg of lamb or roast beef, with an assortment of vegetables in the good old English tradition.

I really believe that his ability to cook basic, wholesome food prompted his move into the restaurant business. At one time he had interests in five restaurants in London and one in South Beach, Florida. They were all wildly successful, with his flagship being Langans' Brassiere in London's Piccadilly.

With his photographic memory, Michael's talent for relating amusing anecdotes saw him in great demand on all the TV talk shows. He held his own against the likes of Johnny Carson and Jay Leno very well. Oh, and during his time in Hollywood he finally got his

With Michael and Shakira at a Hollywood party.

driver's license – at the age of 50! He exclaimed "Now that I've learned how to drive there is nowhere to go!"

As the years passed, and tax regimes eased somewhat, Michael began to get homesick and decided to return to his native England, where he purchased an old mill house adjoining Windsor Racetrack. It was originally part of the monarch's estate and included a back gate allowing him free entrance on race days. If only his father had lived to be able to watch the horses riding down the track from such an advantageous viewpoint – without having to pay for the privilege!

Michael branched out into writing too. Several books along the "Not Many People Know That" lines, listing the strangest facts about show business, were an immediate success. They were followed by *Acting in Film* (an actor's take on movie making) and his autobiography *What's It All About*? They were all written by him, and him alone.

He won his first Oscar for a role in a Woody Allen movie. "Comedy is hard work," said Caine on *Hannah And Her Sisters*, "and Woody, who wrote and directed, understands an actor's problems. While we rehearsed and rehearsed scenes – so many times – he would film each one. I came to the conclusion that the rehearsal was the work and the 'take' was the relaxation. It was brilliant. Woody's attention to minute detail, especially in long takes, paid off handsomely in the final product. He allowed me total freedom with the long passages of dialogue, and also to wear spectacles – maybe he thought I was portraying his alter ego?"

In 1999 I began work on my second Oscar campaign with Michael, for *The Cider House* Rules, and what a joy it was to hear him practice his New England accent with his voice coach.

Advance screenings for the Hollywood Foreign Press Association, Academy members, and the media fully demonstrated that there was a great interest in the adaptation of John Irving's novel, which was centered in an orphanage. The story follows an eccentric doctor (Caine) who has been training a young doctor (played by Tobey Maguire) to be his successor, when the young man suddenly decides to seek a world outside the environment he has lived for most of his life. Even though there was a minor abortion theme which we were worried about, I feel that the deft direction by Lasse Hallstrom enabled us to bypass these concerns and concentrate instead, more positively, on the relationship between Caine's doctor role and the wonderful children.

Michael promoted the film hard in Los Angeles and New York via TV and radio, as well as taking part in many print media interviews.

He went on to win his second Best Supporting Oscar for the film.

"I never expected to win this because the competition seemed too fierce" he later said to me, "and as I climbed the podium to the giant applause I had 15 seconds to think of an acceptance speech."

Michael, Shakira, Oscar and me!

As the audience sat down from their ovation, he proceeded to acknowledge his four competitors by name, saying that the Oscar came to someone without there really being a winner.

He talked about Tom Cruise in *Magnolia*, Michael Clarke Duncan in *The Green Mile*, Jude Law in *The Talented Mr Ripley* and Haley Joel Osment in *The Sixth Sense*, whom he thought was going to win the award. The four of them stood up and applauded, and the audience once again rose to their feet to give him an ovation.

* * *

Of course, Michael remains prolific in his film work. He never stops and has made some terrific movies. Who could forget *Alfie*, *Educating Rita* (for which he was Oscar nominated), *The Man Who Would be King*, *The Italian Job*, *Hannah and her Sisters* (his first Oscar win), *The Cider House Rules* (his second Oscar win), *The Quiet American* (Oscar nomination), *Batman Begins*, and *Youth*?

Michael says the difference between a movie star and a movie actor is as follows: "when the star reads a script he sees how far he can change it to suit himself, whereas the actor sees how far he can change himself to suit the role."

It's easy to see why he is regarded as one of the screen's finest actors of his generation and, damn him, he continues to get better with age!

CANNES FILM FESTIVAL, THE

I have attended many film festivals over the years, and Cannes is by far the most important, and certainly the most glamorous of them all.

Along with the big red carpet premieres hundreds, if not thousands, of aspiring producers and directors manage to scrape together enough money to buy a ticket across to further their visions of artistic merit, and raise production finance. Though most of their planned films never see the light of day!

There is an old saying which goes "I have never known a mother with a cross-eyed baby who didn't think that she had the most beautiful child in the world, and cannot understand why nobody else could see it." The number of screenplays that I have read where I knew there would never be a possibility of ever finding a backer are too numerous to list; of all the screenplays written, less than 5% are ever put into production and less than 10% of those reach profitability. The odds of ever getting a script made into a film are slim to none.

Once a producer overcomes all the hurdles and surmounts these odds, raises finance, and shoots his or her movie, they then need to sell it – advertising and publicity are therefore an extremely important budget item, especially as the movie that can sell itself hasn't yet been made.

The Palais De Festival, Cannes.

Festivals, such as Cannes, prove a very useful launchpad as they offer a unique stage from which we can tell the world about a film.

For over 30 years, since George Barrie first took me to the Cannes Film Festival, I have made an annual trip to the Cote d'Azur and made the small seaside town my home for two weeks in May – publicizing a film or personality.

The Cannes festival has a reputation as being weird and wonderful, as anyone who is anyone (or wants to be anyone) descends and tries to get noticed. Producers pace the Croisette from hotel to hotel, meeting to meeting, in an attempt to raise interest in their scripts. It is one of the few chances they'll have to pitch to Hollywood executives. Companies with completed films for sale engage in all manner of promotion and gimmicks to try and lure you into their screenings. There is a competition going on too, for the prestigious Palme D'Or award. Winning the Festival's top award, or one of the others for Best Actor, Best Actress, Best Director, etc., significantly increases a film's box-office on release. Campaigning is therefore pretty intense!

In 1978 Peter Guber, the executive producer of *Midnight Express*, informed me that the film had been accepted in competition there and wanted a first-rate campaign in the hopes of getting some awards.

The screening of the gripping and powerful drama, based on the true story of Billy Hayes, who was incarcerated for trying to smuggle hashish out of Turkey, and who subsequently managed to escape from the nightmarish prison, was held at the former Palais des Festival where the JE Marriott hotel now stands. There was a 20-minute ovation at the end of the film. I had Billy Hayes and his screen portrayer Brad Davis take bows, as well as John Hurt and director Alan Parker.

The following day the reviews in the trade and general press were overwhelming. We were definitely in with a chance for either best picture or best actor.

Later that week I encountered an old friend, producer Harry Saltzman, who was on the jury, and he told me in confidence that the film would NOT receive any accolades. It seems, in those days, that the jury could be influenced by politics and the Turkish government had – in very strong terms – notified the French powers that be that if they would like to avoid an international incident, *Midnight Express* should be eliminated from any honours. Thus, we came away empty-handed.

I might add that this is very unlikely to happen in today's democratic operation of the festival.

CINEMA PARADISO
Feature film (1989)

This was the first foreign language film which I'd ever represented (it was released by Miramax) and, in my humble opinion, is one of the greatest films ever to come out of Italy.

The story centres on a famous film director returning home to a Sicilian village for the first time in almost 30 years. There, he reminisces about his childhood at the Cinema Paradiso, where Alfredo, the projectionist, first brought about his love of film. It's a moving and very poignant movie.

There was a terrible controversy at the Academy when this was announced as the Italian entry into the Foreign Language section of the Awards that year. The Academy rules state "only one entry from each country, and the accepted film has to have played in its entirety for one week, with paid public admission, in the respective country." An objection was lodged – by an unspecified party – that the film had since been re-cut (and shortened) after its initial release and therefore did not qualify under Academy rules as having been on release in that format. It's a technicality, though one which could scupper a whole campaign!

I set about doing a little research, as I never like to believe so called "facts" when presented by an anonymous party.

Sure enough, I discovered that the longer version was indeed screened for a week, but only as a "sneak preview" to ascertain public reaction. This was not an official premiere of the film and the actual release date was set some weeks later after some re-editing had taken place.

The Academy issued a press release saying it was happy that the film had conformed to the rules – though to my surprise only one trade newspaper carried the story – *Variety*. I felt that without *The Hollywood Reporter*, the other major trade paper, carrying it as well, we would lose a vast number of members' votes, as not everyone subscribed to *Variety*.

I made some phone calls, but to no avail. I then met with Harvey Weinstein, the (then) head of Miramax.

"Harvey I need you to write a letter to the editor at the *Hollywood Reporter*," I said.

"You write it, and I'll sign it," he replied.

So I did. The letter was carried in the next issue and thankfully made everyone aware of the facts – the true facts.

Happily, the Oscar was awarded to the movie.

I'd not actually met Phillippe Noiret, the star of this film (and *Il Postino*, which I also organized the campaign for), though was well aware of him being one of France's treasures — and his Italian is pretty good too! A few years later though, when I was on vacation in Montecatini, I saw him sitting in a café enjoying an espresso. I rarely, if ever, interrupt anyone I don't know, but I just could not resist saying hello and telling him what a joy it was to represent two films in which he starred.

My pigeon French is pretty basic, but mercifully his English is perfect. We sat down and had a long chat and he told me about working on Alfred Hitchcock's *Topaz, Murphy's War, Night of the Generals, Lady L,* and so on … films he'd made in Hollywood. He was and is a lovely, kind, and genuine star – and I use that word sparingly in this business!

COCHRAN, STEVE
Actor

He was without a doubt the oddest actor I have ever represented. Born Robert Alexander, he was a rugged Romeo who vied with Errol Flynn in the romance department off screen. He never made the top ranks, but made films such as *The Damned Don't Cry* with Joan Crawford and *Carnival Story*.

Soon after I began representing him, he held a house-warming party in the Hollywood Hills, and on arrival I was greeted with chickens, rabbits, and dogs which roamed freely in his new abode. With his (new) wife Hedy, he greeted all and sundry – including three of his ex-fiancées – and then his current inamorata went to cook spaghetti in the kitchen.

His death in 1965 was a shocker. Boating was his great hobby and with a three-girl crew he often sailed from Mexico to Honduras and on to Nicaragua. What we didn't not know was he was supplementing his movie income by smuggling gold. He eventually ran afoul of "professionals" in the trade and was stabbed to death on the deck of his schooner far out to sea. The girl crew were unable to control the vessel alone and by the time they were eventually saved by coastguards, his body had started to decompose.

CONNERY, SIR SEAN
Actor, Producer

I was in Spain working as a unit publicist on *The Wind and the Lion* in 1975 with the ex-007, who was trying to emulate his success with Bond whilst at the same time distancing himself from the role he made so famous.

During shooting Sean suggested dinner, over which he hired me as his personal publicist, although our association was short lived – Sean always stated that he never had a publicist or PR representative, hoping that the press would therefore leave him alone. I often wondered whether I was hired because I was representing the then current Bond, Roger Moore?

Sean Connery hired me for a few months before deciding he didn't need a publicist.

We got along well, and I always found him very frank and honest. He never stood for any bullshit, and you certainly knew where you were with him.

COWARD, SIR NOEL
Writer, Actor. Director, Impresario

Frank Sennes booked many acts at the Las Vegas Desert Inn, and amongst them negotiated a deal for Noel Coward for an exclusive engagement at

An audience with The Master, Noel Coward.

the Inn. He decided to have a party for the great Britisher at his Beverly Hills mansion. It was planned for the Memorial Day weekend, and I was worried that many of the luminaries of Hollywood would be out of town for the holiday, but invites were sent out well in advance and the acceptances exceeded our expectations.

Noel arrived, wearing white trainers to accompany his white trousers and multi-coloured sports shirt, and was surrounded by the who's who of show business: Ronald Reagan, Van Heflin, Jean Simmons, Jack Lemmon, Jeanette McDonald, Robert Stack, Gene Raymond, Charlton Heston, Louella Parsons, Fernando Lamas, Arlene Dahl, Jack Benny, Michael Wilding, Robert Cummings, and Greer Garson, to name a few.

For the Desert Inn's first night I persuaded Noel to don black tie formal evening wear, and we arranged a meeting at noon that day, in the desert just outside the city. You see, my thinking was that as he'd written "Mad Dogs and Englishmen Go Out in the Midday Sun" it would be an appropriate photo call gimmick. In fact, that song became not only the soundtrack album cover of "Noel Coward in Las Vegas" but also helped us secure a great spread in *Life* magazine! I was quite proud of coming up with that idea.

D

DICKINSON, ANGIE
Actress

As famous for her role on tv in *Policewoman* as she was in fifty plus years of movies, Angie Dickinson was also noted for organizing terrific poker games!

They were usually held at the home of Ira and Leonore Gershwin on Roxbury Drive in Beverly Hills. Angie was responsible for inviting the guests.

We had the regular gang, which included writer-director Richard Brooks, producer and one time story editor in the great MGM days, Samuel Marx, Tita Cahn, widow of noted songwriter Sammy Cahn; and on occasions the likes of Sean Connery and producer Al (Godfather) Ruddy.

I can't say I ever won much, but for a film buff just being able to sit there and listen to the stories of Hollywood was reward enough. As time passed, several players went to their reward in the sky, and unfortunately Leonore then lost her concentration and our group disbanded.

With Angie Dickinson. I don't think that's me in the painting!

E

EASTWOOD, CLINT
Actor, Director, Producer

Clint Eastwood is not only a highly acclaimed actor, but a most talented director too. His record is exemplary, and whether it be *Dirty Harry* or a Western character seeking revenge or cleaning up a corrupt town, he delivers nothing short of perfection in everything.

I was proudly involved in assisting the Warner Bros. publicity department in the Oscar campaign for *Unforgiven*. Clint won statuettes for Best Film and Best Director. Alas he lost out on Best Actor.

I first met him in 1969 on the set of *Paint Your Wagon*, when I took a trip to the Bishop Oregon location as my client, Jean Seberg (who was playing Elizabeth in the production), was filing for divorce and needed some strategy on releasing information to the media.

Clint and Lee Marvin were having fun under Josh Logan's direction and Alan J. Lerner, who wrote the libretto for the Broadway show, took me on a guided tour of the gold-rush town which had been erected and was going to be destroyed the following week! At the end of the day Lerner gave the lavish sports shirt he had been wearing to a member of the crew – who subsequently told me that the famed writer possessed over 500 of these, and only wore them once. He gave them away on a daily basis.

I next met Clint in 1973, two years after I became a partner with Dick Guttman in our new joint venture publicity agency, on the location of *High Plains Drifter*, which Dick was assigned to.

Clint was directing as well as starring, and his style was very much guided by his earlier work with Sergio Leone, who helmed the "Dollar" movies.

Universal wanted the film to be shot on the studio lot, which would have undoubtedly been less expensive and easier for them to poke their noses in to, but Clint was adamant he wanted a realism about the location, he had a whole town built (and later burned to the ground) in the desert near Lake Mono in the California Sierras. (Where editing of the film also took place – in a log cabin).

Many of the buildings were complete and three-dimensional, so that interiors could be shot there. I think Clint valued being at the fairly remote location as once all the business and budgets had been agreed, he pretty much just wanted to be left alone to get on with the job; he was keen never to waste time. He never went over budget or schedule, so really there was no need for the executives to involve themselves.

Incidentally, in a nod to directors he'd worked with in the genre, look out among the graves in the cemetery for the names of "Donald Siegel" and "S. Leone."

* * *

I guess it was Joe Hyams, Clint's personal publicity representative at Warner's, who first involved me on a film with Clint, as it was felt it needed special handling. *White Hunter, Black Heart* – based on the making of John Huston's *The African Queen* – which was not the "typical" Eastwood kind of film fare.

The story was set in 1951, with film director John Wilson (Eastwood) casting for his latest project about a hard-drinking boat captain and a school teacher who take on the German Navy in Africa during WWII.

In real life, Huston was obsessed with shooting an elephant during the making of his film; in fact, he chose his locations – the most inhospitable ones you can imagine – because of sightings of elephant herds in the area.

Mirroring real life, John Wilson takes the big pay check to clear his debts, while hoping to fulfil his long-time dream of going big-game hunting. Writer Peter Viertel had been on location with Huston and recorded his experiences, on which the Eastwood script was based.

The film was well received when shown at Cannes, although it was not a box-office success. Clint stopped work on his next film, *The Rookie*, for five days, in order to attend the festival, at an estimated cost of $1.5 million.

While at Cannes with me, Clint fulfilled a life-long ambition by meeting Akira Kurosawa, director of *Yojimbo*, on which *A Fistful of Dollars* had been based.

* * *

Clint's knowledge, both in front of and behind the camera, is tremendous. He is truly an icon of Hollywood. He knows what works and what the cinema-going audience will be interested in, and also knows he has to deliver his projects within a reasonable budget if the backers are to make a decent return.

When executives of the major studios decreed that the "Western" genre was dead in the 1980s, Clint put down his *Dirty Harry* Colt '45 and gave us *Pale Rider*, followed soon after by *Unforgiven* – demonstrating that there was indeed an audience for the genre. Clint had the power to convince a studio to back him that no other actor did. The genre certainly would have been dead if it wasn't for Clint.

Working on the Oscar campaign on the latter film was a particular joy for me. With my then-partner Dick Guttman, the plan was to create a soft-sell campaign, because Clint is very uncomfortable with publicity. You are not going to see him suddenly appearing all over the media expressing how great his movie is. The idea was to subtly make it appear to the press that they were discovering his new project and talent as a director and to give it and Clint some visibility without it being overly-obvious what we were in fact doing – selling a picture.

With Clint Eastwood at the Oscars. He kindly inscribed this photograph.

I established a relationship with Wombat Productions of New York to produce a documentary biography of Clint, shown on Cinemax cable. In addition, a one hour interview with British veteran interviewer David Frost revealed the personal side of his charismatic personality, and this was subsequently shown around the world on TV.

Clint was always a little uncomfortable being interviewed, as I think he saw it as a distraction from work, plus the press were always more interested in his private than professional life. Nevertheless, he was very candid in the Frost interview – perhaps one of the few times he has been.

One of my cherished possessions is a photograph taken with Clint just before the Oscar ceremony, while ushering him through the throng of photographers at the Dorothy Chandler Pavilion in 1992 for *Unforgiven*. He subsequently signed it with the inscription "To Jerry – Many thanks for the great night – Clint."

* * *

In 1994 Clint filed against the *National Enquirer* for invasion of privacy and appropriation of name and likeness. I was called as a witness for the Central District of California trial, which related to an exclusive interview that the *National Enquirer* purported Clint had given them on becoming a new father. It would have been very easy to ignore the scandal publication, but on principle he was determined to prove that he never gave such an interview.

On the witness stand, the lawyers asked me how I was so sure that he never met the journalist involved. I stated "In all the years I have worked with Clint, it would be over his dead body should he ever allow himself to be in the company of a representative of such a paper, let alone be interviewed."

The jury took little time to decide on their verdict, finding for Clint on three claims for relief under the Lanham Trademark act and awarding him $150,000. Several weeks later I received a plastic cube paperweight from Clint, decorated with the front page of the *Enquirer* together with a copy of the complaint and the jury verdict Form!

EDUCATING RITA
Feature film (1983)

Without doubt, this film was Michael Caine at his very best. He had absolutely nothing in common with the character he was playing – a drunken old English college professor – yet shone.

Not a lot of people know (to coin a phrase) that he grew a bushy beard and added 30 pounds so as not to obviously convey any possible romantic notions towards his student (Julie Walters). He was keen that their relationship didn't develop into "an old man chasing a young woman" one, which could have easily come across.

The director, Lewis Gilbert, took the script to all of the major Hollywood studios. Most of them were interested; several even admitted to loving the script, but they all wanted American leads. I know Burt Reynolds and Dolly Parton were suggested at one point.

Lewis packed his bags and returned home to London. They just didn't get it! He was determined to cast a relatively unknown actress named Julie Walters, who had played the part of Rita in the stage play – which was wonderfully written by Willy Russell – and wanted Michael Caine for the male lead. He pressed ahead alone.

Then John Dark came on board as producer, got the money together, and a distribution deal was struck with Columbia.

Michael says he drew on his friendship with Robert Bolt, who had once been a teacher himself, to flesh out his character.

On the first day of shooting at Trinity College in Dublin, Michael said he spotted a familiar face coming towards him. As the chap got closer, Michael realized that he didn't know him at all, but the reason he was familiar was because "He mirrored the way that I looked – he was overweight, had a straggly beard, his face still flushed from the last night's drinking, and to top it all, he was carrying a case of red wine." Michael stopped him and asked, "You wouldn't be a professor of English by any chance would you?"

"As a matter of fact, I am. How did you know?" he asked.

Michael smiled and said "Just a lucky guess."

Initial fears about casting Julie Walters, who had never been in front of a camera before, were soon wiped from everyone's mind as she delivered the performance of a lifetime.

About two weeks into filming, Lewis said to Michael "I think you and Julie will get Oscar nominations for this."

He was right, they both did – though alas lost out on the night.

[see also **CAINE, MICHAEL SIR**]

FAREWELL MY LOVELY
Feature film (1975)

After some years of having stepped back from unit publicist work – in favor of supervising publicity and orchestrating release and Oscar campaigns – mainly because I could no longer afford to be away from my office for weeks and months at a time, I received an invitation from producer Elliot Kastner. He asked if I would be unit publicist on *Farewell My Lovely*, which was set to film entirely in Hollywood.

Dick Richards was to direct and, incidentally, had a young promising assistant named Jerry Bruckheimer, who has risen to become one of Hollywood's most successful producers. He assured me I would be able to work for a few hours on set and then get back to my office to write copy, telephone the media, and get home to my wife at night. It sounded ideal.

Charlotte Rampling and Robert Mitchum were cast in the lead roles. I had met Miss Rampling previously in London, and this was her first picture in Hollywood. She was without doubt one of the most cooperative stars I have ever encountered. She never grumbled once when we needed photographs or had members of the press on set to interview her.

Robert Mitchum I was a little unsure about. He had a reputation, as they say! What I didn't expect though, was to spend every lunch time in Robert Mitchum's trailer listening to the most fascinating stories of his career. He did a wonderful impersonation of John Huston, with terrific articulation, as seen in *Heaven Knows Mr Allison*, describing problems with the various World War II locations. On another occasion, he talked about his experience in Ireland when working on David Lean's *Ryan's Daughter*. For some time, from the start of shooting, he had tried to get the director's attention by asking if he could have a private conversation, but was continually rebuffed because Lean was encountering production problems and didn't need an actor adding to his worries. Fair enough, Mitchum thought, be like that. Finally though, Mitchum managed to get the director to himself, and tactfully told him that he was wearing the wrong costume. Thus, many scenes had to be reshot.

I did see the other side of the actor though – to the gentle, unassuming raconteur that I shared each lunch time with – when, one day, the director Dick Richards presented Mitchum with new script pages, which were for the following day's filming. In front of the whole crew, Mitchum proceeded to tear it to shreds.

"I agreed to appear in this remake of Raymond Chandler's mystery," he said, "based on the script I was handed, and I never agreed to rewrites."

Being the major star, he won the war of words and they filmed the original lines.

FINCH, PETER
Actor

I first encountered Peter Finch while I was representing Robert Aldrich on *Flight of the Phoenix* in 1965. We were in the Arizona desert shooting in 110 degree heat with only a simple tent to save us from sunburn.

Peter was most affable as we sat down to discuss his segment of publicity, and I could see why he was a favourite of Robert Aldrich – he was an easy going, terrifically nice guy.

One day during the shoot, Peter called across to me "Jerry, what are you doing in May?"

I shrugged my shoulders.

"How about joining me in Rome for a holiday and some fun?"

I don't think I'd ever been invited to spend a weekend away in the States, let alone a holiday in Europe. I usually took a little time off in May, so said "sure." It wasn't one of those empty promises, he really meant it. I duly arrived in Rome, was met by Peter at the airport, and so began a tour of nightclubs, chic restaurants, tourist destinations – he took me everywhere. He never wanted anything in return, and was quite simply the most generous host you could ever want.

Sadly, I had to wait three years to work with Peter again. That was on a more controversial film, *Sunday Bloody Sunday,* where he played a homosexual psychiatrist. He was terrific. A wonderful actor, and his moving closing speech, made directly to the camera, remains a masterpiece of understated delivery.

United Artists opened the film fairly low key, in New York, and didn't expect any great things – a homosexual love story was not really regarded as something society would accept in their droves. However, they were wrong. Outstanding reviews flooded in. The LA opening was announced as being the next week and John Schlesinger, the director, and Peter were in great demand on the media circuit. Both were nominated for Oscars.

Peter Finch was brilliant in *Network*.

From time to time, when he was making a movie in California, Peter would rent a house in Beverly Hills. He'd always make a point of calling me and invited me over for dinner, or at the very least a drink. When in town to make *Network* in 1977 he spoke about it being the role of his life – playing tv newscaster Howard Beale on the brink of a mental breakdown – and his portrayal was the talk of the town.

Sadly, he died soon after completing the film – far too young. He was the first actor to ever to receive a posthumous Oscar.

FINDING NEVERLAND
Feature film (2004)

This enchanting film came about when director Marc Forster heard about the story from his agent.

"He'd found the script and sent it to me, and this was just before I started *Monster's Ball*," Forster told me "and I loved it. After we finished *Monster's Ball* I was told the script was still available, and they just decided I could do it".

They shot on location in London and at Shepperton Studios, and Johnny Depp was cast as JM Barrie (the creator of Peter Pan) and delivered one of his most understated and finest performances.

Its 2003 release date was pushed back because of a film directed by PJ Hogan hitting cinemas.

"Contractually we could not compete with the *Peter Pan* movie" Forster explained to the press. "We had to wait for over a year to get our's released."

In fact, it was due to a deal Miramax had struck with Columbia, who were producing the Pan movie, and owned all film rights to the character. In exchange for allowing our movie to recreate scenes from Barrie's original play, Columbia stipulated there had to be a year between the two films' release.

Realising it was very much a movie for all ages, I arranged a huge number of family screenings for the Academy members. It was wonderful to see the screening rooms full of three generations of families in many instances. I'd like to think more voting members got to see it because their children and grandchildren nagged to be taken. Happily, our campaign paid off as it secured a number of Oscar nominations – including for Johnny Depp and Kate Winslett, as best actor and actress.

In the event, the magnificent score by Jan A.P. Kaczmarek took the film's only Oscar.

FIRST MONDAY IN OCTOBER
Feature film (1981)

When I was asked if I'd be free to take on this project I wondered what the title referred to – but didn't want to make myself look foolish by asking the producer! So, I did a little digging around and discovered it refers to the U.S. Supreme Court's first session of the new season.

Henry Fonda had been offered the role of the crusty liberal Justice, Dan Snow – a character based on William O. Douglas, which he had previously played to great acclaim on stage. Jane Alexander was cast opposite him on stage as Ruth Loomis, the first woman Supreme Court Justice – and a very conservative one she was. The two characters are at constant odds with each other.

Ronald Neame was signed to direct. Producer Paul Heller got the finances together, and then Fonda dropped a bombshell. His daughter Jane had asked him to make *On Golden Pond* with her and he was therefore no longer available for this movie.

Ronnie Neame immediately contacted Walter Matthau, who was very wary.

"That's Hank's [Fonda] part. I wouldn't do it unless he tells me it's okay."

Henry Fonda was very gracious and gave his blessing to Walter Matthau, who read the script and commented it seemed "wordy."

The producer responded "They're good words though, don't you think?"

"They're Academy Award words as far as I'm concerned" replied Matthau.

It was unfortunate that a film about the Supreme Court was not allowed to film at the actual location. They granted permission to shoot on the steps, but nowhere inside, so an exact replica was constructed on a movie stage – from a series of stills of the courtroom interior.

Jill Clayburgh was now suggested for the female lead, fresh from a best actress nomination for *Starting Over*. The cast was set and a bidding war took place between the studios for the distribution rights, with Paramount being the victor.

All seemed rosy, but then disaster struck. The Screen Actors Guild called a strike, which was to last 95 days. Then Jill Clayburgh announced she was pregnant, and it was agreed the schedule would be altered to accommodate her, though alas in pre-production we received news that Jill had miscarried.

Michael Eisner, then head of Paramount, was naturally informed. Bear in mind that he was Jill's cousin, when I tell you that his sole response was "I'm closing the picture down." He didn't bother to ask how she was.

Paul Heller refused to respond to this knee-jerk reaction and continued – the plug wasn't pulled at all, it was just Eisner over reacting.

Matthau wasn't without his health problems. After recent heart surgery he was forbidden to go up higher than eight thousand feet. This presented a problem when we needed to film a sequence on a mountain covered in snow – there just wasn't any at eight thousand feet. We needed to go higher and defying his doctor. Walter volunteered to go as high as was needed. In fact, he only had to climb an extra 500 feet, and lived to tell the tale.

The main thrust of the story, and the case for which the two justices appear in the Supreme Court, was about a pornographic film called *The

Naked Nymphomaniac. Paul Heller actually engaged an "adult film" company to produce 10 minutes of footage for our use, but of course it wasn't to appear in the film, as we didn't want that sort of certificate imposed – it was a comedy, not an "adult" movie. Ronnie used it skilfully in playing it on monitors in the court, but only filmed reactions to it!

Critically, it was a success. Financially, it wasn't. This was the era of *Star Wars, Indiana Jones*, and other big budget action adventures. This type of movie just wasn't in favor. Alas.

FORMAN, MILOS
Director

A native of (then) Czechoslovakia, he was undoubtedly one of the world's great directors; and it was my good fortune to be hired by him personally to attempt an Oscar campaign for *One Flew Over the Cuckoo's Nest*. The reviews, of course, were great, though the competition even greater!

One always studies the opposition when campaigning for "Best Picture" and here we had "Jaws", "Dog Day Afternoon", "Barry Lyndon" and "Nashville" all of which had equally great critical acclaim.

Directors Steven Spielberg, Sidney Lumet, Stanley Kubrick, and Robert Altman were formidable opponents – I realised I'd need a strategy pitched above the merits of the directing alone.

In conversations with Forman, I discovered that the Russians could play a great role in my attempts to woo Academy voters. You see, 1975 was a year that the Soviet Union controlled Czechoslovakia. Consequently, its citizens were unable to travel abroad without special permits, and Milos told me, as he was now an American resident, he could visit his family there but they were not permitted to come to the U.S. – and in particular, not able to join him for the Oscar ceremony.

I leaked stories to the news wire services, newspapers, and columnists, and hoped that the excitement of the Academy Awards would create a softening of the Soviet's position on Milos' family, while of course heightening awareness of the director and his terrific movie. Even the American ambassador entered the fray!

It wasn't until ten days before Oscar night that we heard permission had been granted. It had worked! The news made headlines all over again, and the whole voting period had been dominated by Forman's plight.

He went on to win the Oscar, and for my part he gave me a very generous "thank you" check.

Along with Best Director, the film also won statuettes for Best Picture, Jack Nicholson won for Best Actor, Louise Fletcher won for Best Actress, and Lawrence Hauben & Bo Goldman won for Best Screenplay. Not since *It Happened One Night*, some forty-two years earlier, had a movie won all five major Academy Awards.

G

GAMBIT
Feature film (1966)

Ronald Neame was signed to direct this light-hearted drama, with Shirley MacLaine in the lead role. Though there remained the question of the male lead.

Shirley had just seen *The Ipcress File* and suggested its star, Michael Caine, be considered. He had, of course, the year before been Oscar nominated for *Alfie*. He was immediately offered the role.

I remember there was quite a problem with Shirley MacLaine's make up on this film – to achieve the Eurasian look as described in the script, her eyes were taped back, but under the heat of the lights the tape kept coming loose. It was a constant problem throughout the day, which really frustrated Ronnie and resulted in us losing valuable time – in fact, over the course of a few weeks, the production fell behind by two days.

The studio executives were becoming itchy, as they realised it was now costing them money, and started making noises. Ronnie, not to be fazed, told them point blank: "The reason we are behind is because of Shirley's eyes. Remove that problem and we'll be back on course."

They did, and Ronnie got back on course.

Another, more amusing moment during filming came with the introduction of the Universal Studios tour. It was big business guiding people around the lot, and an exciting opportunity for film fans to catch a glimpse of movies in the making and, if there were lucky, a film star. At certain times throughout the day we would hear one of the guides passing by … "on your left is Michael Caine's dressing room, and on your right we have Shirley MacLaine's dressing room".

Shirley became ever more exasperated each time she heard him, and decided to change the name on her door to "Zelda Glutz."

Michael wasn't too pleased either – feeling a bit like a monkey in a zoo. However, he bit his tongue and didn't complain. Just as well really, as that young guide was a chap called Michael Ovitz – he became Hollywood's most powerful talent agent and later signed Michael as a client!

Gambit was a fun and successful comedy heist movie and really put Michael on the map in Hollywood. It also generated buzz around awards season and secured three Oscar nominations in the technical departments for Best Art Direction, Best Costume Design and Best Sound.

A remake came out in 2012 starring Colin Firth and was a complete disaster – proving some things really ought to be left alone!

[see also **NEAME, RONALD**]

GARNER, JAMES
Actor

My five years with Jim were not the easiest. This in no way is a criticism, but because he just hated publicity, and in particular talking about himself. It was like pulling teeth to have him meet with the press, but whenever he showed up journalists loved his sense of humor, and his easy-going manner.

Whenever I had anything to discuss, or rather anything to try and persuade him to do, we generally met at the Bel Air Country Club – where he played golf at every available opportunity. I once managed to talk Jim into doing a *TV Guide* cover story, but when it appeared in print he called me up saying he was very upset. You see, they'd mentioned he had a problem with his knee, and Jim regarded it as a negative story. He gave me quite a hard time about it, but I hadn't been the one who told the journalist he had a bad knee – Jim did that himself.

Anyhow, to try and placate things I arranged

The easy going Jim Garner.

to meet him for lunch a couple of days later, and prepared to apologize profusely – even though it wasn't of my doing.

However, far from meeting a frosty client, I was greeted by him beaming widely. It turned out he'd been talking with Jackie Cooper, the former child star and now prominent director, who'd said "Jim, this is a great piece because it shows your humanity together with the fact that, like the rest of us, you have the odd physical ache and pain."

Jim liked that and I became his best friend again!

GIBSON, MEL
Actor, Director, Producer

Freddie Fields, a former agent, was a neighbor of mine, and we used to share a coffee and chat occasionally about what was going on in town and who was on the way up (or down). One such day over coffee in the early 1980s he told me that he was making a career change into production and hoped we might be able to work together in the future.

After producing *Looking for Mr. Goodbar* and *American Gigolo* at Paramount in 1983 he was appointed president and COO of MGM Film Co. and United Artists.

He telephoned a week later and asked me to lunch at the studio to discuss my overseeing one of his forthcoming productions. I was given the option of selecting one (of a number of films on their slate) and chose *The Year of Living Dangerously*, which was set to star a young actor named Mel Gibson. Freddie also told me, in confidence, that the role of Billy Kwan would be played not by a male, but by diminutive New York actress Linda Hunt. He saw an opportunity to deceive the media and public as long as possible.

Well, the truth behind the casting had broken in the Philippines when a journalist for the *New York Times* wrote a very flattering piece describing the makeup and costuming of Linda Hunt. Linda's mesmerizing performance led to suggestions of an Oscar nomination as Best Supporting Actor or Actress, and that's where I came in – to construct a campaign around her role.

I took the film to Cannes and we staged a magnificent party on the Carlton Hotel Beach, and that really served as our launchpad for the months ahead leading up to voting time. Incidentally, she won the Oscar for Best Supporting Actress.

Meanwhile, I'd spent many hours with Mel Gibson and got to know him quite well. I could see he was very much an actor on the rise, and seeing an opportunity to assist in that, asked if he had any thoughts about a personal publicist. Well, it seems I was very opportune in asking, as he was indeed thinking along those very lines and asked me lots of questions – in fact, we chatted for several hours as he picked my brains. He asked if I could put a proposal together that we could discuss as soon as we were both back in LA, and that he'd call me.

Weeks went by after my return home without a phone call from Mel. I thought maybe he'd misplaced my number, so I put a call through to his agent at I.C.M., who happily informed me that Mel had interviewed several publicity agencies in Hollywood and had since made his choice.

Not even so much as a thank you or even "kiss my ass!"

GOLD, ERNEST
Composer

Like most great musicians and composers, Ernest Gold was nearly always working, but not always earning much. So when he asked me to represent him he apologized that he couldn't really afford to pay me, but suggested an arrangement whereby I would receive 5% of his gross earnings; in a bad year I wouldn't earn much at all, whereas in a good year I stood to do reasonably well. There were more bad years than good!

As time passed Ernest went from scoring independent movies (which paid him a minimal fee) like *The Screaming Skull* to being producer-director Stanley Kramer's resident composer.

Then one day in 1960 Ernest took me to lunch and said he'd been signed by Otto Preminger to score *Exodus*, and for the first time in his career had been hired six months before principle photography was due to commence. By industry standards, that was extremely rare. He researched ancient music and themes and came up with a score that was so phenomenally popular it almost replaced Hatikvah as the Israeli national anthem!

Praise came from all quarters. Ernest was riding high and definitively in with a chance of an Oscar. We realized that the front-runners he would be pitted against included four of Hollywood's giants: Dimitri Tiomkin for *The Alamo*, Andre Previn for *Elmer Gantry*, Elmer Bernstein for *The Magnificent Seven,* and Alex North for *Spartacus.* Between them they took so many full-page advertisements in the trade papers that it became quite ridiculous.

I decided to go the other way, and take only one. The copy was clean and showed the Exodus symbol next to very large type: "JUDGE THE MUSIC—NOT THE ADS. Music by Ernest Gold."

I was delighted when Ernest won the statuette. There couldn't have been a more deserving winner.

Building up to the ceremony, Ernest kept thanking me for organizing his campaign and was so pleased with the way it was all going. Well, that was my job. The day after the ceremony Ernest came by my office and said he had a gift for me; I hadn't expected anything, but when he produced a very cheap pole lamp I really wished he hadn't bothered. I never judge a gift by its monetary value – it is the thought that counts – but Ernest clearly hadn't put an ounce of thought into it. It looked very cheap – and this was in appreciation of my work? It should have told me something.

After a chat, I brought the subject round to my 5% fee. I hadn't received anything all year, and had a feeling if I didn't mention it there and then I might not hear anything from Ernest. My instincts, alas, proved right.

He said "You know I haven't worked since last October so there is no money."

I couldn't believe it.

"What about the great success of the soundtrack album?" I asked, which was topping the charts everywhere.

He then said that I did not share in his record royalties.

Our previous deal of 5% of gross income suddenly excluded record royalties?

"Why would I work for five months if I was not going to be compensated?" I asked. I was more annoyed to think I had marketed his gold album as an adjunct to the campaign too.

Coining a Rolling Stones great hit that I was getting "no satisfaction" I decided, for the first time in my career, to seek an attorney.

Nine months later, on December 27, I received the news Ernest had offered to settle out of court.

Needless to say that was the end of our professional relationship, but several years later we met by chance. I couldn't let the moment pass without saying, "Why, Ernest?"

"I felt that I didn't need a publicist, as I had just won the Oscar, was famous the world-over and believed that the work would come to me."

He subsequently realized that unless your name is constantly in the media, those who hire talent soon forget who you are. Hollywood is fickle like that.

GOOD WILL HUNTING
Feature film (1997)

I thought "This isn't the greatest title for a film!" when I heard it was one I was asked to represent for the Oscar campaign.

Two young actors, Matt Damon and Ben Affleck, were fed up of scratching around trying to get work. An actor's life is never easy, but they realized that they stood a better chance of finding a script they could both star in if they controlled it – i.e. wrote it. That's exactly what they did.

It was rumoured that studio script doctors lent a hand – William Goldman being one – but even if that is the case, it's still a remarkable debut for two young actors turned writers.

Damon excels as the title character, a hardworking but rebellious Boston boy, nearing 21 but with no life plans other than getting wrecked and picking up girls with his best mate (Affleck). Only he's also a mathematics genius!

When Skellan Skarsgård's professor discovers this, he's

determined Will should fulfil his potential. Forced to attend therapy with a bereaved psychiatrist (Robin Williams) or be sent to jail, Will must face up to his traumatic past if he's ever to have a future.

Williams is subdued but likeable, while Damon makes his implausible character totally believable. Gus Van Sant's unobtrusive direction simply leaves us to enjoy their burgeoning friendship.

It was a terrific film to work on and I really sold the "two actors turn writers" angle. It won the hearts of the voters and the two boys walked off with Best Original Screenplay statuettes.

GRANT, CARY
Actor

It was George Barrie's igloo style Brut office in Manhattan where we were planning a trip to Sun Valley for one of my more outlandish promotions – a "Brut Film Festival" – that I first met Cary Grant. Brut Productions had only made four features by that time, and whilst they were not doing it

Cary Grant was a huge talent on both sides of the camera.

in an effort to be honored by their peers, they did feel transporting their stars to this luxury beauty spot for a spot of PR wouldn't harm efforts in trying to attract filmmakers for future projects.

Cary Grant was most enthusiastic – he was a director of Brut – and through him we were able to attract some of Hollywood's great talents to join the celebration, and so began my first collaboration and meeting with him.

I subsequently travelled with Grant on the Los Angeles to New York flight several times and was always amazed how rarely we spoke; he always took a window seat and just before we started down the runway he would say "Good night" and be asleep in seconds. Five minutes before landing he would wake up. After a few trips, I asked how he managed to fall asleep so swiftly.

"After 30 years of flying I know how to relax and will myself into a state of euphoria. And besides, I escape the inane conversations of fellow travellers."

That told me!

One rumor about the actor that prevailed for years was about how tight he was with money. I never experienced it, but choosing my moment, one day asked him. He told me he was staying at the Plaza Hotel in New York and ordered two English muffins for breakfast. Room service arrived, but under the silver platter Grant noticed there were three half muffins. He called the manager of the hotel who explained that they had just had an audit done by an efficiency expert, and it had been calculated that, on average, residents consumed one and one third of a muffin. Cary's replied was that as the other half of his muffin was therefore consumed by another guest in the hotel, he wouldn't be paying for two and that they dare not put it two on his bill.

A telephone operator was listening in to the conversation and soon spread word of the actor "being cheap!"

Grant also told me he never said "Judy, Judy, Judy" – which has always been impressionists' favorite line in impersonating him. He never bothered to refute it publically because, he said, "at least it kept my name alive."

My favorite story relating to Grant is the famed one of the *Newsweek* reporter who sent a telegram to the Brut offices saying "HOW OLD CARY GRANT?" – obviously for an article he was writing. Grant was in the office, picked it up, and duly replied by wire "OLD CARY GRANT FINE."

With so many outstanding pictures to his credit, it's amazing to think he was only Oscar nominated twice, and the only statuette he received was an honorary one in 1970. Rex Harrison presented the award and said: "In our business they refer to the new Cary Grant, the Oriental Cary Grant, the European Cary Grant, but there is ONLY one real Cary Grant…"

I echo that.

GREEN, JOHNNY
Composer

I was told I'd easily recognize Johnny Green, the head of MGM's music department, on my first day at the studio's publicity department, as he was most conspicuous with a boutonnière in his lapel.

When I visited his office to introduce myself, sure enough he was easy to recognize, and told me that he would supply me – any morning I'd like it – with a bagel and cream cheese, a hot cup of coffee, and news of any composer castings on productions. These he wanted planted in the Hollywood trade papers immediately.

Johnny maintained a great seriousness about his work and rarely cracked jokes. A Harvard graduate and accomplished pianist, he made his break in the entertainment field by becoming accompanist to two Broadway luminaries: Ethel Merman and, subsequently, Gertrude Lawrence. At the same time his song writing career blossomed with such hits as "Body and Soul," "I Cover the Waterfront," and "Out of Nowhere." This led to his forming his own orchestra in night clubs and on Broadway. In 1949 after years of composing and conducting, including for the *Jack Benny* radio show, he was appointed general music director and executive in charge of all music at MGM studios. There he went on to win three Oscars.

There was much friendly rivalry in his department, as assignments to films were made at his discretion.

My main job for Johnny was, as I mentioned, planting stories in the two Hollywood trade papers, making sure that I never played favorites – Johnny was most insistent about that. Though he had great confidence in his team, Johnny would usually reserve the most prestigious films to work on himself.

After my departure from MGM into the independent world of publicity I received an urgent call from Johnny, asking me to have breakfast at his Beverly Hills mansion. He was more serious than ever and said it was about making a major announcement to the press. I couldn't imagine what was more important than ever, and when I arrived he rambled on for ten minutes before reaching the point. He had decided to change his name!

"Why after all these years would you want to do such a thing?" I bellowed.

He took another ten minutes to describe his recent meeting with "Buffy" Chandler, the doyen of the Music Center of Los Angeles – who also controls the Hollywood Bowl. She had apparently said that if he was to ever conduct the Los Angeles Philharmonic he should be known only as "John Green." For why, I don't know.

We discussed it further over breakfast, but he was adamant; so I arranged an announcement to be made to all media. The irony of the situation was that he waited another two years before he was allowed to conduct at the Bowl!

Not long afterwards he left MGM and went on to win two more Oscars for *West Side Story* and *Oliver!,* but his career unfortunately took a turn for the worse when speculation and rumors of his wife's association with the Moral Rearmament cause broke. Tinseltown turned its back on Johnny. For all of its magic, creativity, and glitz, Hollywood also has a dark side I discovered. Here was the most creative composer and arranger in town (*An American in Paris, High Society, Raintree County*) being ostracized. It had nothing to do with his work or anything he'd done. It was purely down to his wife's political sympathies. In later years we used to meet at director Jean Negulesco's house, but Johnny (as I still referred to him) was partly paralyzed then and confined to a wheelchair. Sadly, we knew it was only a short matter of time before he would depart this world – having never really forgiven Hollywood.

GREYSTOKE: THE LEGEND OF TARZAN
Feature film (1984)

One of my great friends in the industry is producer Stan Canter, who struggled for years to put together a movie called *Greystoke: The Legend of Tarzan, Lord of the Apes.*

The first version of the script was written by Robert Towne, but just before production cranked up there was a dispute. Towne wanted the sole

110 • *Jerry Pam*

credit, but Stan had since brought in another writer – Michael Austin – to work on the script, and therefore he would have to share the credit. Bob Towne was furious and took the matter up with the Writer's Guild, saying he wanted sole credit, or no credit at all.

The Writer's Guild ruled that Austin contributed significantly and was entitled to a screenwriting credit, but added Bob Towne didn't have to be credited if he didn't want to be. Often, in cases like this, people assume the name "Alan Smithee" for their on-credit, but Towne chose the pseudonym P.H. Vasak.

To everyone's amazement, the screenplay was nominated for an Academy Award.

Although I wasn't assigned to the film I unofficially worked behind the scenes for it to win.

The reason was not so much to assist the producer or Towne, but more of an attempt to get Vasak to walk down the aisle to the stage to accept his award.

Why? Well Towne had used his dog's name for his credit!

Sadly my efforts failed and we didn't get to see the pooch take to the stage.

GUNFIGHT, A
Feature film (1971)

Harold Jack Bloom was a writer of such films as *The Naked Spur* (with James Stewart and Janet Leigh), and TV shows *Bonanza, The Man From Uncle* before working on the James Bond film *You Only Live Twice.*

In 1970 he'd written a screenplay called *A Gunfight* and had the idea that Native Americans would finance it. It is a story where the two lead characters, Will Tenneray and Abe Cross are gunslingers past their prime, and both are broke!

Bloom managed to raise $2 million from the Native Americans – perhaps keen to see two aged gunslingers shoot it out? With the money in the bank, he persuaded Kirk Douglas to play Tenneray and convinced popular country singer Johnny Cash to make his film-lead debut as Cross.

I don't think Bloom quite knew which of the two gunslingers should win though, and consequently he filmed two endings – with each being killed. The paying public was then asked to vote which of the characters they'd like to see killed in what was thought to be a novel idea for movie-going.

It didn't prove that popular – the public going out for an evening of entertainment like to be told a story, not have to decide on how it ends. So much so I don't think the idea has ever been tried again.

I believe the Native Americans lost their two million by the way.

H

HAND, THE
Feature film (1981)

Oliver Stone was an up and coming director, and quite well known writer (particularly of *Midnight Express*). He'd written a script called *The Hand*, which was all about a cartoonist who loses his hand in a car accident. The missing body-apart then takes on a life of its own and starts killing people. It didn't really sound like a project Michael Caine would ever be interested in, as were the rumours about Stone's ideal casting, but what do I know – the phone rang and Michael told me that he'd agreed to star. I asked him why?

"It's a horror film and I've not done one before, and the young director impressed me so much that I wanted to be a part of his team," he replied.

Fair enough.

Though Michael found working with Oliver Stone a fascinating experience, he simply did not enjoy the physical process of making a horror film and said he'd never do another. I'm not sure Michael particularly likes blood and gore to be honest. It thoroughly depressed him in fact.

One thing Michael shared with Stone was that they were both ex-infantrymen. Conversations often centered on their experiences in the field and Stone said that he hoped one day to make a film about his time in Vietnam, and tell the real story of that war. *Born on the Fourth Of July* was that film, eight years later.

Thankfully the commercial failure of *The Hand* did nothing to hinder either of their careers.

HARRIS, RICHARD
Actor

One of my most colourful clients was blond Irishman Richard Harris; looking after him was no mean feat! The cantankerous thespian, who could be charming one minute and vitriolic the next, challenged one's dedication to the art of the reasonable.

I'd heard all the wild stories relating to his drunkenness, even to his reportedly stealing a London bus, which he totalled near Hyde Park in London – resulting in his being banned from driving. I don't know if he was better or worse for later giving up the drink; certainly his mood swings didn't alter.

In fact, I asked him why he had suddenly stopped boozing and was amazed at his answer.

"I was so fed up listening to stories of what I was supposed to have been doing, like getting into fights and having affairs – none of which could I remember. I finally decided that after 25 years I couldn't live a life being unaware of what was happening to me."

In 1978 Dick Guttman showed me a script he had written. It was good. Very good. Having talked through ideas about who we might send it to and where we might raise finances, we realized that our having represented so many actors, directors, and productions ourselves (Dick was a publicist too, with whom I'd recently joined forces), we were in a pretty strong position to try and package it. What's more, we'd own it 100% and wouldn't just be the hired publicists.

Had we even imagined the trials and tribulations with which we would have to contend, we wouldn't have bothered! A producer's role is many fold: in raising finance, negotiating with agents, casting, securing a director and so on. That's just for starters.

We approached and received positive replies from Michael Caine and

Richard Harris, the eternal charmer.

Jaclyn Smith regarding the lead roles and the noted British director Ronald Neame. As time passed, and as our financing wasn't yet in place, these talented individuals signed for other projects – they had to keep paying their bills after all.

We realized that Harris – who was arguably a bigger name then – could replace Michael Caine, Beverly D'Angelo could replace Jaclyn Smith, and that we should take advantage of the tax shelter financing in Canada that everyone kept telling us about. In adding native talents like Christopher Plummer, Kate Reid, and Saul Rubinek in featured roles, and with director Peter Carter – who was regarded as a landed immigrant north of our border – we met the criteria.

William Immerman, a lawyer and former executive at Twentieth Century Fox, became our partner and line producer and with the backing of Robert Opekar, a Canadian oil producer, we secured co-production finance. Filming was scheduled to start in Toronto. At last it was all coming together.

Just prior to principal photography Harris informed me that, as Dick and I had to publicize him in our movie, he saw no reason why he should continue paying us our regular agency fee. It seemed a very petty, especially in spite of our getting him a $750,000 salary – an outstanding fee in 1979.

Highpoint, as it became titled, turned out to be one of the low points in my quest for making a successful motion picture. Matters were not helped when director Peter Carter refused to participate in a publicity campaign we'd organized in Los Angeles before shooting commenced – that should have been an omen.

The production had its share of ups and downs, but then catastrophe hit! The climax of the story involved a fall from the Canadian National Tower in Toronto. We hired Dar Robinson, one of the world's great stunt artists, for the sequence. With a parachute tucked under his suit, he doubled for Chris Plummer, who was to hurtle to his movie death 1100 feet below. With a very tight schedule and a budget fast running out, we only really had one take at this scene. With that in mind six cameras were brought in to ensure coverage from every possible angle of the fall. We weren't taking any chances!

Despite our best endeavours and intense planning only one camera functioned. Five, for one reason or another, failed to capture the most important sequence in the movie.

By this time, we were losing the light and the weather was changing. We simply could not reshoot and certainly didn't have the time or money to think about coming back the next day.

Highpoint was a bit of a low point actually.

In an attempt to try and save what we could, it was decided to convert part of the fall to slow motion and cut away to a few close ups, but this failed miserably and we lost the dramatic intensity we so needed.

With a major photograph of the fall planted in *Newsweek* and two pages about it in the *National Enquirer*, movie critics who anticipated something very exciting at the previews just yawned at the final product. After a limited release, the film landed on HBO cable.

Following the debacle, a disappointed Richard Harris went back to Britain and I didn't have any further dealings with him – until about twelve years later.

By then, Harris' career had been in a bit of a slump, but when he signed on to make a low budget Irish drama called *The Field* in 1990, it was to undergo something of a renaissance.

The word on the film was very positive, and in particular Harris's performance was singled out. He therefore felt he had a pretty good chance of being nominated, and contacted me to attempt an Academy campaign on his behalf.

He arrived in LA for the press screenings, which went very well, and we arranged to meet up at the Sunset Marquis Hotel near the Sunset Blvd. strip, for a publicity planning conference. Richard knew that after years of being overlooked by the top movie casting directors, and with only a few mediocre TV movies under his belt in recent years, his star was finally rising again. Though he perhaps put a little too much importance on winning the Oscar...

One of the things he asked me to do was take a two-page advertisement in the Hollywood trade papers with the reviews of the movie on the left-hand page and the reviews of a play, in which Harris had recently triumphed in London, on the right. I explained the latter had absolutely nothing to do with his movie and only serve as a distraction, but he wouldn't listen. I stood my ground though and firmly told him that if he wanted to win for *The Field* then he had to concentrate his efforts on that movie – and not a play, thousands of miles away in London. Quite frankly, who would care? After days of arguing, I finally won the point.

A nomination for the Best Actor Golden Globe, from the Hollywood Foreign Press Association, was a good start to our efforts. Though, in typical Harris style, he decided to fire me at the celebration dinner, hosted at the Beverly Hilton afterwards, because he wasn't sitting at a ringside table! Faxes churned out of my machine, accusing me of not adhering to his wishes. I was quite blunt with him in my responses, and really didn't want anything more to do with him.

A few weeks later the Oscar nominations were announced. Harris was named one of the Best Actor nominees. I knew even Richard Harris had a conscience and would be embarrassed by his behaviour towards me, now that he'd secured the prize he so lusted after. For all of his arguing and ideas he must have realized I had a point, but it took him one week to swallow the pill and call me. He said that he was sorry and MAY have been a little too hasty.

I truthfully knew that – at very best – his chances of winning the Oscar were slim. But irrespective of his winning, my campaign was orchestrated to convince the powers-that-be in Hollywood that he was still a fine actor. It worked! In the decade following his nomination – and despite him not winning – his career went from mediocre to A-list. He starred in *Patriot Games* with Harrison Ford, *Unforgiven* with Clint Eastwood, *Gladiator* with Russell Crowe, and two *Harry Potter* movies to name but a few. Of course, he wouldn't have got any of those gigs had he not an immense talent, but I like to think I helped a tiny bit.

Incidentally, I must tell you about an amusing incident which occurred at the annual Oscar nominee's lunch. It is an opportunity for all the people singled out in all the categories to meet and exchange pleasantries, and is preceded by a press conference. At that conference Harris announced, at the age of 61, he had finally decided to portray "Hamlet" onstage and one wag shouted out "Who's going to play your mother?"

Harris, in his typical bravado way, did not react kindly!

HARVEY, LAURENCE
Actor

Larry Harvey was one of the classiest actors in Hollywood. He was born in Lithuania and grew up in London where he became a star, before taking Hollywood by storm. His appearances in *The Alamo, The Manchurian Candidate*, and *Room at the Top* (for which he obtained a Best Actor Oscar nomination), are just a few of his outstanding features. He was also bisexual and, unlike many other leading men who feared it might damage their careers, never hid that fact. Mind you, he'd been married to British actress Margaret Leighton, Harry Cohn's widow Joan, and finally Pauline Stone, with whom he had one daughter (born whilst Larry was still married to Joan!); so the press probably had enough to write about him without digging into his other affairs. Though many rumours circulated that his long-time lover was British film producer James Woolf, I never asked Larry about his personal life, taking the view that ignorance was my best line of defence if I was ever quizzed on the subject by the media.

I represented Larry's PR interests over several years and always relished visiting his lavish pad just off Coldwater Canyon in Beverly Hills, to discuss strategy on upcoming films. I was never in any doubt that this very talented and intelligent actor was destined for great things, but tragically during the shooting of Brut Productions' *Night Watch*, with Elizabeth Taylor, he was taken ill with severe stomach pains. He was diagnosed with advanced cancer.

I visited him in hospital in London and remember he asked if I could send him some "True Blue" cigarettes when I returned to the States. He'd always been a heavy smoker, but a fastidiously fussy eater believing a healthy diet was the key to longevity. He was particularly outspoken at his horror in developing stomach cancer, but refused to stop smoking despite the doctor's advice, not believing it could be a contributing factor.

His death in November 1973, aged just 45, was certainly a tragedy.

In their obituary, the *New York Post* described Larry thus … "cigarette dangling impudently from his lips, Laurence Harvey established himself as the screen's perfect pin-striped cad."

I'll second that.

HELP!
Feature film (1965)

[see **BEATLES, THE**]

HEPBURN, AUDREY
Actress

Being the entertainment editor of a daily newspaper at the beginning of my career gave me access to some of the most famous people in Hollywood; there were those who were more famous than others of course – Audrey Hepburn being one, and readers relished reading about her.

I remember Roger Moore telling me that his long friendship with Audrey stemmed from a TV commercial they made together in the 1950s for a skin cream called Valderma.

"She brought an incredible honesty to any role she played," Roger said, "because she was a very honest person. Film acting is what is going on behind the eyes. In her case, they were fabulous eyes too."

Having a word with Audrey Hepburn and Henry Mancini.

I remember writing when Gregory Peck signed for *Roman Holiday;* he thought the picture was all about his character. But when he and Audrey shared a scene for the first time he realized it would be very much her film. He said to the director, William Wyler, "She has to have billing over the title – she's going to win an Oscar for this."

She did.

Audrey Hepburn was relatively unknown at that time, she'd only had smalls part as a match seller in *Laughter in Paradise,* as a ballet dancer in *The Secret People*, and one line in the Alec Guinness comedy *The Lady Killers* before Wyler tested her.

Before the opening of *Breakfast at Tiffany's*, publicist Gerry Sherman and I were assigned – by Paramount Pictures – to purchase radio advertising on stations around the U.S.; we were consequently invited to see a preview of the movie and were also played tracks from Henry Mancini's great score including, of course, *Moon River*. Mancini revealed that after a sneak preview in San Francisco, one of the chiefs at Paramount wanted the song dropped from the movie as he didn't think it worked. Mancini stood firm and said "Over my dead body." What a good thing he did!

Despite her great success, Audrey Hepburn never got big-headed. She once told me, "The miracle of my career Jerry, is that I was in Hollywood working with four of filmdom's greatest directors – Billy Wilder, William Wyler, Fred Zimmermann (*The Nun's Story*), and Stanley Donen (*Two For The Road*)."

A later starring role on Broadway in *Ondine* garnered her a Tony Award and a year later she married her costar Mel Ferrer.

After 1967's *Wait Until Dark*, Audrey stepped back from acting and decided to concentrate on her family and charity work. Nine years later she was persuaded to return, with Sean Connery, in the critically acclaimed *Robin and Marion*. Although she made a couple of subsequent movies, in 1988 she became a UNICEF Goodwill Ambassador and devoted the rest of her life to the cause. Not many people realized that she herself was a UNICEF child – saved from the brutalities of the Nazi regime, along with the poverty and malnutrition that ensued in her home country.

She simply said "I want to give the children hope."

Roger Moore, who later became involved with UNICEF through Audrey, related that "she gave the children joy and care, and never revealed the true horror and upset she felt through witnessing their often tragic problems."

Four years before she passed away, Steven Spielberg cast her in a small role as an angel in *Always*. How fitting.

HIGH ROAD TO CHINA
Feature film (1983)

Take the High Road to China... for an adventure you'll never forget.

So said the tag line. Does anyone remember it? I thought not.

Tom Selleck was a jobbing actor who hit the big time with a tv series called *Magnum PI* in 1980. *High Road to China* was his first feature film

Tom Selleck in *High Road to China*. A High Road to Nowhere would have been a better title!

lead-part; and he was tipped for the big time, though one or two good career choices were overshadowed by many bad ones, and he never really did make the A-list.

The film was directed by Brian G. Hutton of *Kelly's Heroes* and *Where Eagles Dare* fame, and was in fact Hutton's last film as he chose to bow out of the film business at the age of 48, having invested heavily in real estate with enough money to live the rest of his life comfortably.

Courtesy of the production, I made my first ever trip to the former Yugoslavia. I can't say it was a very enjoyable experience! It wasn't a particularly easy location to work in, and hotels were pretty basic to say the least. I think someone on the crew described it as "the armpit of Europe". A very apt observation.

I remember at one point in the high action, explosive packed adventure yarn, they ran short of … explosives. That was a bit awkward to say the least when most scenes featured something blowing up. Up until very recent to our arrival the communist republic had been ruled with an iron rod by President Tito for 35 years, and such items as dynamite were not readily available to a visiting film crew! In fact, had Tito still been alive, I'm sure we'd never have been allowed to film there.

And so we waited for a UK production manager named Peter Manley to arrive, with his two large suitcases of clothes and, hopefully, the answer to our problems. Just how he managed to get through customs I'll never know, but a rather sweaty, red-faced Manley was delighted to meet his driver at the airport to hand over his luggage – which was in fact packed with high explosives!

Shooting recommenced.

Alas, that was probably the most excitement I can report on the movie. It was, if all told, a dud.

HITCHCOCK, ALFRED SIR
Director, Producer

I only met Alfred Hitchcock once. That was at the annual British American Chamber of Commerce Annual Christmas Lunch.

Being on the board, I was expected to secure the "Man of the Year," so I wrote to the director and to my delight and surprise he responded positively, but on one condition – I had to write a speech and set them on cue cards

Sir Alfred Hitchcock (here with one of the stars of *The Birds*) was our Man of the Year.

for him. He also said that his health had been failing recently and he would need a wheelchair to transport him from the parking lot to the dining room.

I thought about the speech for some time, and just didn't know how to start it. I didn't want it to be over-sentimental, appear egotistical or, dare I say, boring. After discarding many failed attempts, I came up with the idea of using his film titles.

At 1:30pm, following lunch, Mr. Hitchcock stood up and – after taking his applause – said his most famous line:

"GOOD EVENING."

With roars of laughter he continued:

"When I first heard that I was to be honored at this annual ritual, I discovered that it was more difficult to find the location of this event than any of the pictures that I have done throughout the world. It seems the Century Plaza Hotel is unlisted so I called a friend who turned out to be THE WRONG MAN who told me to go NORTH BY NORTHWEST and without a SHADOW OF A DOUBT you will find the hotel. He must have been a SECRET AGENT because it was SABOTAGE. Maybe he had STAGE FRIGHT or maybe he was for THE BIRDS. In my FRENZY I realized THE TROUBLE WITH HARRY was that he was THE MAN WHO KNEW TOO MUCH. I CONFESS having been SPELLBOUND by his lack of knowledge. I had the SUSPICION that it would take more than 39 STEPS to find this room. Rather than being called a PSYCHO I got in my car, opened the TORN CURTAIN, looked through the REAR WINDOW and found this NOTORIOUS hotel."

He received a rapturous applause and I smiled widely knowing I hadn't messed it up!

HOFFMAN, DUSTIN
Actor

I only represented Dustin Hoffman once, in 1978, when he filed a lawsuit against First Artists Corporation over a violation in his contract giving him "final cut" on two motion pictures in which he starred: *Agatha* and *Straight Time*.

His lawyer contacted me, and after discussing various PR strategies in his office, he arranged a meeting with Dustin at the Westwood Marquis Hotel. On arrival, Dustin's first question was "Why do I need a press agent?"

In those days there was a prevailing con-

With Dustin Hoffman.

temptuous attitude by several New York newspapers towards Hollywood, and I reasoned that as litigation was about to take place, a good public relations campaign would certainly help his cause and would prevent him being painted as the villain of the peace by the other side.

I arranged interviews in the *New York Times* and *Variety* and began to sense warmth emanating from the business for Dustin, which in turn he responded well to and opened up. I think he realized how a good media relationship benefitted him, and he won the case.

The following year he also won the Best Actor Oscar for *Kramer vs. Kramer*.

HOWARD, TREVOR
Actor

I was in my late teens when I first met this handsome British leading man on the set of Ronnie Neame's *Brief Encounter* in the late 1940s. He was starring with Celia Johnson and being directed by David Lean, while I was applying for a "Youth in Training Apprenticeship" with the J. Arthur Rank Organization. Alas that apprenticeship never materialized due to a lack of funding – nothing changes in the film business!

Many years later, in 1956, our paths crossed again in Hollywood. I'd noted, in the *Hollywood Reporter*, that Trevor had arrived at the Hollywood Roosevelt Hotel to prepare for his co-starring role with Jane Greer in *Run for the Sun*. The hotel was somewhat archaic and had not had any restoration so, on a hunch, I called him, and after introducing myself as a fellow Brit and with many mutual friends in common, I suggested moving him to the Beverly Hills Hotel where he would be much more comfortable and more able to "associate

Trevor Howard was a lovely man, and a fellow cricket lover.

with the powers of Hollywood." He liked that idea. During our chat I mentioned cricket – of which I was a great fan, as was Trevor – and I think that sealed our friendship.

After moving, Trevor was awestruck by the service and soon recognized what he had been missing. Unfortunately though, one of his drinking buddies, Robert Newton, soon found him and in no time they were partying

And just to prove the point, here I am playing cricket!

and singing rowdy songs along the corridors at 3am. By 7:30am they were packed and booted out of the hotel! So much for my good deed.

In fact, I received a frantic telephone call seeking my assistance in securing a new hotel for them both, and let's just say I was so glad when he flew off to Mexico a few days later to start the film, as we started running out of hotels they weren't booted out of.

Years later I was at the Cannes Film Festival and while walking along the Croisette I espied Trevor being interviewed by a TV journalist. I stopped to observe and when he caught sight of me he jumped up and rushed over – neglecting the fact that he had microphone wires attached to his chest! – he asked me to join him at the table and immediately started discussing cricket. The interviewer must have wondered who the hell I was and soon became very impatient, eventually suggesting I leave and see Trevor later.

We agreed to meet for dinner that night at the Carlton Hotel and brought ourselves up to date on our respective happenings, and our mutual appreciation of cricket! His dedication to the sport was so great that he often flew to Australia to see England in their annual battles for "The Ashes" a symbol of over 100 years of rivalry.

HUGHES, HOWARD
Producer, Director

I met the reclusive Howard Hughes on two occasions back when I was an entertainment editor at my paper, and was amazed at his shyness and reticence in meeting members of the press. Normally, Hollywood moguls liked nothing better than to get their name and face in the papers. Our first meeting was rather embarrassing actually, and took place at a hot dog stand in Santa Monica where I was "stalking" him. Well, not quite stalking…I happened to be meeting a columnist from the *Los Angeles Herald Express* named Jimmy Starr – who was famous for drinking ten vodka and orange juices at one sitting – and he suggested we meet in Santa Monica, where one of the Hughes Aircraft facilities was based, as he wanted to show me where Hughes would partake of a snack at lunchtime.

At noon we were munching on a superdog at a stand and the man himself came over, but went inside the lone telephone booth situated next to the stand for what seemed like an eternity. We waited and waited.

Finally he presented himself at the counter, whereupon the owner started to curse him out.

"How dare you monopolize the phone every day you show up here. I am losing customers because of you and I do not want you around here anymore."

Hughes rapidly departed to his gigantic acreage across the street.

I received a phone call when I returned to my office, from Starr, informing me that another telephone booth had been erected on the other side of the hotdog stand within the hour. Such was the mysterious tycoon's power!

My second encounter followed an invitation from RKO Studios to go to Las Vegas for the premiere of *Las Vegas Story*, starring Jane Russell (who was under contract to Hughes) and Victor Mature.

On arrival we were bussed from McCarran Airport to the hotel for an early dinner, followed by a screening of the movie and a press conference, with the stars of the feature in attendance. At that time the only flight back from Vegas was at 2:00am – the casinos wanted guests to gamble as much as possible and not sneak out of town early – However, Hughes met us in the bar and said that we would leave at 10:30pm for the airport. Nobody could understand why he'd arranged the early call, but we trundled on to the busses, and within ten minutes of our arrival a TWA Constellation landed. We boarded.

A passenger, who sat alongside me on the return flight, started shouting to the stewardess: "When I boarded in Chicago they told me this was a non-stop flight to Los Angeles, so why the hell did we stop in Vegas?"

The answer soon became very clear. Hughes owned 74% of TWA and the boss himself had ordered the plane to touch down on our behalf. When he bade us farewell he never mentioned this fact.

Years later I was asked to handle the Oscar campaign for a film directed by Martin Scorsese called *The Aviator*, which was all about Howard Hughes. In an odd way I felt as though I was more qualified for this particular job than anyone else. The film went on to win five of the eleven Oscars it was nominated for.

HUSTON, JOHN
Director, Actor, Writer

Born in Nevada, Missouri – yes there is such a town – John Huston travelled so extensively in the U.S. with his journalist mother during his formative years that he felt it instilled in him the "fantastic desire to become a world traveller."

His first movie as an actor was in 1932, in the Universal Western *Law and Order*. However, it was directing that really appealed to him and, in 1941 he took the helm on *The Maltese Falcon*. George Raft was offered the lead role of Sam Spade, but said he didn't want to put himself in the hands of a first-time director. The role was offered to Humphrey Bogart and the rest, as they say, is history.

I mentioned that it was really through watching John Huston's *Moulin Rouge* that I became captivated and intent on working in the business. Never did I realize that one day I would not only be in Hollywood, but be working in publicity on several of Huston's films! He even spent time with me socially on occasions. Furthermore, he invited me to guest in a poker group that he founded, but the stakes were too high for my modest salary.

It was in 1966, in Cairo, that we first met during his helming *The Bible*, when I was visiting my client Stephen Boyd, who was starring in the "Tower of Babel" sequence. He invited both of us for cocktails in his suite at the newly constructed Shepherd's Hotel (the old one burned down), and I was as timid as a mouse! To see this towering and dynamic personality in the flesh was awesome, let alone to be drinking cocktails with him.

It was clear, in no time, that his charm, witticisms, and eloquence were enough to seduce anyone who was in contact with him.

It wasn't until nine years later that our paths crossed again when I was assigned, by the now defunct Allied Artists, to publicize *The Man Who Would Be King*, which Huston was again directing. Of course, I avidly read all the biographical notes on his background, together with the articles and newspaper column stories of his travels and filming throughout the world. Some have said that he was the "eccentric's eccentric." Certainly the numerous tales of his drinking, gambling, and affairs of the heart made him sound like a person who loved life and had a life many of us would have loved to emulate.

During luncheon breaks he would often regale the cast with some of his adventures and share anecdotes from his previous films. For 25 years Huston had tried to put this short story by Rudyard Kipling together as a film, but was continually frustrated because the cast – the bankable names – he needed always seemed to elude him. In what turned out to be his (almost) last attempt in the mid 1950s, he was able to get his great friend Humphrey Bogart to say yes. This was a coup of short standing because the other role was then accepted by Clark Gable — a few months later, Bogie died of cancer.

The Man Who Would Be King finally made it to the big screen with Connery and Caine in the lead roles

There was great difficulty in finding a replacement of such magnitude and Huston forgot about it and went on to direct *The Misfits*. It was then Gable asked about the possibility of resurrecting the film. Alas, very soon after, Gable – another true giant of the silver screen – succumbed to a heart attack and the film was again put aside.

Huston thought about the possibility of another try in the mid 70s and realized that the movie-going public had become more sophisticated, and would no longer accept American stars portraying British soldiers. In 1975 it was announced that Sean Connery and Michael Caine had accepted the roles. It was a terrific coup to cast them together, and their on-screen chemistry was magical.

Huston famously never "directed" actors; not that Michael or Sean ever grumbled, you understand. But when a reporter asked Huston about his technique he said "I am a better casting director than a movie director. If you cast correctly, the actor knows the role and acts accordingly."

Michael Caine echoed this when he told me, emphatically, that Huston was the best casting agent in the business. "Whenever I had a problem, John would just say that he cast me because I was right for the part and I should just relax."

Following our association on this movie I then met Huston again in 1979, when I was assigned to take his finished print of *Wise Blood* to the Cannes Film Festival. I created a poster which depicted just his head in the character he portrayed in the film. His film of a drifter searching for sin who becomes a preacher was well received by the critics at the festival – but not by the public. It starred Brad Dourif, Ned Beatty, and Harry Dean Stanton, with Huston playing the grandfather character (the one in my poster).

We met several times at the festival's famed Hotel Du Cap to discuss the film's campaign at Cannes. He would often talk – and I was quick to prompt him to at any opportunity I was given! – about Humphrey Bogart and the four films they made together. An amusing tidbit concerned his directing the Warner Bros. wartime drama *Across the Pacific*, which starred not only Bogart, but Mary Astor, Sydney Greenstreet, and Huston.

Just about the time he was finishing up on the film, he was served his call-up papers to enlist in the armed service. The penultimate scene he shot was with Bogart trapped in a house surrounded by Chinese soldiers. How was Bogie to escape? Huston said it wasn't his problem! He never finished the scene and the problem was left to Vincent Sherman to fathom out.

Wonderful!

One of the saddest moments in his life also concerned Bogart. Their last meeting took place at Bogie's house in Beverly Hills. The screen legend was using the dumbwaiter to descend from the second storey and was then wheeled into the lounge. "He was obviously dying and had lost a tremendous amount of weight" said Huston sombrely "but he was determined for us to have drinks as a farewell. That was the image that has stayed with me all these years."

Without a doubt Huston had one of the most fascinating lives and careers in Hollywood, though he was never really happy being a part of "Hollywood life," and chose to spend 25 years living in Ireland migrating, he said, "to get serenity away from the bustle of Hollywood," and indeed also to become a horseman once again.

I was fascinated – and so lucky – to hear of all the people he had met. He was a modest man with it. He loved movies and making them. He wasn't hung up on fame and credits. Quite the opposite. I recall him saying that he once visited Ernest Hemingway in Havana; the great novelist did not know that Huston adapted his *The Killers* short story for the movie without credit – not for any political reason, but purely because this would have revealed that he was moonlighting while on another movie! He later received credit with another writer, Anthony Villier.

I'll forever remember Huston talking about Marilyn Monroe, "At the Fox commissary lunch for Nikita

Khrushchev, she arrived 15 minutes early for the first time in her life. I said 'Obviously the Russian President is the only person to direct her next movie.'"

I

IL POSTINO
Feature film (1994)

Sadly, eighty percent of foreign films never see the light of day outside of their native country unless they get an Oscar nomination; yet, so many are better than our native offerings.

When I was asked to handle an Oscar campaign for the movie, I of course went to see it, and was immediately bowled over. I said it would be a treat and honor to represent this intelligent and touching story with its remarkable performances.

Not to be confused with the Kevin Costner film, *The Postman*, released around the same time, this is a far superior movie in every respect. It's a charming Italian-language tale of a meek and mild postman who befriends famed exile, Chilean poet Pablo Neruda. The title role was played triumphantly by Massimo Troisi, and he in fact received a Best Actor nomination – one of the very rare occasions a foreign film received such a plaudit. Additionally, the film was also nominated in the Best Picture category, making it something of a sensation.

Troisi was actually very ill at the time it was made, and in fact persuaded producer Vittori Cecchi Gori to fast-track the movie and hire noted British director Michael Radford. Troisi saw it as a role of a lifetime, though his life was marked because he desperately needed a heart transplant. Alas, just 12 hours after completing principle photography he died, at the age of 41.

I'm so proud to have helped the movie gain the recognition it richly deserved and feel the greatest sense of accomplishment for my campaign on it, above all others I've worked on.

IRONS, JEREMY
Actor

"I couldn't think of anything else to do" was Irons' response to my genuinely inquisitive question of why he chose to go into the acting profession during our first meeting. It endeared me to him greatly and I found him to be a consummate professional with a rare honesty about himself.

In 1981 he achieved great success in the tv drama *Brideshead Revisited*, and five years later was cast as one of the main leads in *The Mission*, opposite Robert DeNiro. At the time of production, Britain was at war with Argentina (where the film was shot) and that presented all manner of complications, not least in having the producer, David Puttnam, smuggled in and out without the authorities knowing!

I was asked to handle the Oscar campaign for the movie, and in interviews Jeremy admitted it was the toughest thing he'd ever been associated with – with inhospitable locations and constant trekking over rough terrain, plus his co-star.

"Working with DeNiro was most difficult in the beginning," he admitted "and it wasn't until I discovered the director Roland Joffe seemed to cast characters who react against each other, then the penny dropped in how I should approach everything, and DeNiro in particular. We later became great friends."

IT'S A DOG'S LIFE
Feature film (1955)

Of course, for every blockbuster I worked on there was an occasional a dud. MGM publicity chief Howard Strickling would often assign publicists to what he termed "problem films" – films which required a more creative form of exploitation. That is to say, films that they knew were real turkeys but needed to try and attempt to get some of their money back on! One such (low budget) feature was *The Bar Sinister*, also known as *It's a Dog's Life* – starring a four legged K9.

I've always enjoyed a challenge, so I arranged a press preview and for the star of the film, a pit bull terrier, to sit in the box office at the theater, welcoming the critics. In fact, I had an assortment of dogs, of every breed you can imagine, lined up as if to pay for tickets to enter as a photo opportunity. Inside the theater I then sat (with a little cajoling and a few treats) as many dogs as I could in the front row, as if they were viewing the film with a regular audience. The media loved the photo opportunity and the hundreds of press clippings testified to their interest. There was certainly a bit of a buzz about the movie, though perhaps a little too much as it landed me in court for violating the health codes of Los Angeles! No pets are allowed inside public buildings.

Luckily the judge, being both a movie fan and dog lover, only admonished me and dismissed the case.

Sometimes I did wonder if I was a little too smart for my own good.

The film lost the studio $850,000, proving once again that you can't really dress up a turkey as anything but a turkey.

J

JACKSON, GLENDA
Actress

Glenda Jackson took Hollywood by storm with *Women in Love*, and I knew she would have a great chance of winning an Oscar, and the remarkable reviews she received from the nation's critics further underlined my belief.

United Artists, the film's distributor, had a problem though – the title. Some thought it suggested lesbianism, and we knew how *The Killing of Sister George's* box office was party hindered by the censors imposing an adult rating because of "lesbianism." You can appreciate UA were anxious to maximize its investment from a wide audience, so I suggested as it was based on DH Lawrence's famous book, could we perhaps check as to how widely read and available it was in the States? They did a little research and discovered that was a significant public awareness of the book (and that it was not at all a story of same-sex relationships), so it made sense to build on, and take advantage of that – they stuck with the original title.

The film was lauded by audiences and Glenda became the toast of Tinseltown, winning her first Oscar as Best Actress. The following year she triumphed again with an Oscar nomination for *Sunday*

With Glenda Jackson.

Bloody Sunday, and in 1975 she secured another for *Hedda*. I worked with her on the latter and on *A Touch of Class* (which I've written about earlier, see **BARRIE, GEORGE**), and those two campaigns really were both a joy.

Glenda retired from acting in the late 1980s to pursue a political career and, for many years was very active in British politics as an MP. In the last UK General Election (in 2015) she retired and stood down, and has since dipped her toes back in acting again.

JANSSEN, DAVID
Actor

He was a man's man who was extremely successful in TV, though remained frustrated that all his movie roles were unmemorable; he never quite became a "movie star" even though he appeared in more than 35 films. *The Fugitive* established him as the definitive TV series star and that's what stuck.

Friday lunches were important in David's life, as he loved to get away from his Century City apartment. We would meet at Ma Maison – the hangout for many of the luminaries of show business – and it was there that he offered to sell me his Rolls Royce Corniche convertible, distinguished by its unique golden colour. Years later, in 1980, I drove to his funeral in this magnificent car and parked outside the chapel where the service was being conducted. Stan Herman, a realtor friend of David was shocked to see the Rolls at the funeral parlour, thinking that David had still owned the automobile and had driven it to his own burial!

The car was also the center of conversation at a dinner party given by gossip columnist Rona Barrett for Lucille Ball and her husband Gary Morton. All through the evening Gary kept talking about the gold Rolls parked outside, and finally he said to me "Where did you get that car?" I replied that I had bought it from Janssen, and he exclaimed "I knew I had seen that car before. It had caught fire in Palm Springs and David had to order a new engine from England." I then mused that this was the reason why I got such a great deal from my erstwhile client.

Sadly, David's only real "decent" film role came in his final year. He'd enjoyed a major part in *Inchon*, but due to the film's release being delayed for years – because of the political backing by the Korean Rev. Sun Moon – it was decided to cut his part in an attempt to present the film as having just been completed. Hollywood has a philosophy, based on past experience, that if a film is completed and is not released for a year or two then it must be non-commercial and therefore disappointing. Not true! Thus David's best movie role has never been seen. A great shame.

K

KENNEDY, GEORGE
Actor

During my association with director Robert Aldrich I discovered he liked to engage a few "regulars" in his cast lists. One such character was George Kennedy.

In 1966 George had appeared in the Warner Bros. feature film *Cool Hand Luke* with Paul Newman, and for the first time in his acting career there seemed a likelihood that George could achieve some critical success if he played his cards right – and maybe even an award.

I had been working on Aldrich's *Flight of the Phoenix*, which starred James Stewart, with Kennedy in a featured role, and during our many weeks on set George and I would chat. Of course he discussed *Cool Hand Luke* with me, and asked if I would represent him for a campaign; he certainly felt he had a good chance of snagging an Oscar nomination. The buzz on his performance in the film was admittedly very good, and we shook hands. I then formulated ideas which included interviews, column items, and trade advertising. George was more than happy, and very willing to participate in anything I felt would boost his chances.

My first layout was a photograph of Kennedy from *Cool Hand Luke* with the headline: "KENNEDY IS THE NAME TO WATCH." I felt that his name, being the same as Senator JFK who was then running for the presidency, might create some talk within the industry. George felt my approach was a little too blatant, so I devised a one page advertisement which consisted of a photograph from the movie – of George holding up a battered Paul Newman who had just been beaten up by prison guards – with, across the top of the page: "GEORGE KENNEDY *SUPPORTING* COOL HAND LUKE." Obviously, using the word "supporting" referred to the Oscar category which we were trying to achieve a nomination in.

Nomination day duly arrived and the announcements went as follows:

John Cassavetes for *The Dirty Dozen,*
Gene Hackman for *Bonnie and Clyde,*
Cecil Kellaway for *Guess Who's Coming to Dinner,*
GEORGE KENNEDY for *Cool Hand Luke,*
and Michael J.Pollard for *Bonnie and Clyde.*
George came over to my office, overjoyed. He said

"No matter what happens at the Academy Awards I will be with you for the rest of my career, Jerry".

Comforting words for any publicist!

Oscar night arrived and George, smiling widely, won! There was a terrific celebratory dinner afterwards, and George invited me to be a part of it. I felt a firm friendship had been forged.

How wrong I was!

The following day we left for San Francisco to promote his new film *Flight of the Phoenix*. On arrival at the Fairmont Hotel I went to his room to make sure all was well and he was just opening his suitcase. To my astonishment he pulled out the Oscar, and stared lovingly at it. It was then, at that moment, I realized that my days were numbered. His expression said it all – it wasn't just one of pride, but of total, and I mean TOTAL self-conceit.

George was certainly very full of his own importance during our publicity tour; he was an Oscar winner and felt he should behave like a star – but real stars don't change with success, do they?

A short while later I found that I could not get in touch with my "client." He was always out when I telephoned, never returned my messages, and never came by the office. Finally I managed to track him down and asked what the problem was. He said that his friends felt he needed a "breath of fresh spring air." In other words, it was "Thanks Jerry, but I don't need you any more, I have all I need"; but he wasn't honest enough to say that.

The night George Kennedy won his Oscar and our friendship was sealed – or rather doomed!

I had half expected it to be honest, and while I was upset, especially as I thought we were friends, I decided it best just to walk away. He clearly didn't need anyone to help him, let alone guide his media profile in Hollywood. He'd chosen a few good projects to follow his Oscar success, so good luck to him I thought.

Years passed, and in 1980 I was representing the very popular *Merv Griffin Show* on TV. One night I learnt that George was going to be one of his guests. When we met in the green room I asked the obvious question "Why did you do it?"

His reply startled me. "Because I was crazy and felt that with an Oscar I was set for life."

On the show he praised me to Merv and afterwards said that he would have rehired me, and would do now, but he had too many financial troubles.

The man I met that night was the old George. I was sorry to hear he was experiencing money problems, and could not help but wonder if there was something I could do to help.

The following day an idea came to me. I realized I might be able to get him a role in a movie I was representing that was about to move into production, *A Rare Breed*, concerning the kidnapping of a famed racehorse belonging to Texas millionaire Bunker Hunt. I knew there was a part in there perfect for George that hadn't been allocated. I called the producer, Jack Cox.

I played it cool and nonchalantly asked Jack if the casting had been completed – knowing full well it hadn't – and he said that he was struggling with finding the right actor to play the horse trainer, Nathan Hill. I said "How would you like an Oscar winner for the part?"

He thought I was crazy.

I assured him I wasn't and George was hired for $150,000.

Feeling quite proud of being able to help my old friend, I called him to ask if he'd like my professional services again, as mentioned on the Merv Griffin Show. I tactfully suggested he hadn't had many decent roles in the last few years and this one, if handled correctly, could see him garner a bit of positive publicity and boost his profile again.

"Jerry, didn't I tell you I was deeply in debt?" he said.

I replied yes, but I'd just helped him land $150,000 and his debt would have been much larger without my assistance. I didn't ask an agents commission – though I would have been entitled – I just thought he was being honest about wanting to take me on again if he could afford to. But obviously, his loyalty did not lie with anyone but himself. He hadn't changed. That was the last time we ever spoke.

L

LANCASTER, BURT
Actor

I was involved on two movies with Burt Lancaster and have to admit both were very unsatisfactory in terms of commerciality and the actor's attitude!

I was dealing with an actor who hated publicity, and whose mantra was "My work speaks for itself. The public pays to see me and I give them a performance, and that should be enough."

You might say my presence was therefore superfluous. I often wished it was – but the producers begged to differ!

Castle Keep was a World War I drama about American soldiers occupying an ancient castle filled with objets d'art. Marvin Linktner, a very professional photographer, was hired to develop some advertising art and also supply stills for national magazines. Marvin was an additional photographer, known as a "special" and was engaged to work alongside the unit still photographer for a specific assignment. He and Burt became fast friends and played chess whenever there was a pause in the filming. Though, for days Burt would cross his arms against his face and say "no shots" following each scene.

After a week, which was the time allocated for Marvin's work, Marvin left with no photos of the star. Our planned major campaign thus fell rather flat! The duly film never reached its full potential despite a great supporting cast of Peter Falk, Tony Bill, Bruce Dern, and Jean-Pierre Aumont.

The other movie rejoiced under the title *The Hallelujah Trail*, and was one of the Mirisch Company's poorest efforts. Set in the Old West, it concerned a wagonload of whiskey which is waylaid by Native Americans. The comedy western was directed by John Sturges, five years before he gave us *The Magnificent Seven*.

On the first day of shooting Burt said to me "Do NOT ask me to do anything to support this film as this marks the completion of my long-term contract, and I was forced to do this inept script to gain my freedom."

Needless to say, I never even bothered!

Once again, we had great supporting cast which included Lee Remick, Martin Landau, Brian Keith, and Jim Hutton – and so I concentrated my publicity efforts around them. Though the media and public aren't stupid and know if the star of a movie doesn't get involved in its promotion, then it spells trouble – and usually a pretty mediocre film.

Alas I was fated to be associated with a great actor, who I'd so admired from afar, on two of his weakest films.

LAST TANGO IN PARIS
Feature film (1972)

When your lead actor is Marlon Brando you might think publicity will be a dream job. It certainly is not! Like Burt Lancaster, Brando was one of the most un-cooperative people you could possibly ever meet. His philosophy, gain, was that his work speaks for itself, and he would never engage in any promotion or publicity. Period.

This film, an erotic drama, shocked most of those who saw it – nowadays the sex scenes are probably pretty tame in comparison to much of what we see, but back in 1972, it was quite a thing.

I, fortunately, had the complete opposite of Brando in female lead Maria Schneider, and it was with her that I put together a campaign – though I have to admit that word of mouth was probably our most valuable asset on this movie.

Many were quick to call it pornography, but we chose to publicize *Last Tango in Paris* more as a great exploration of cinema's visual possibilities, with Bertolucci's sensuous, erotic, and thought-provoking use of the camera throughout the film. The final ballroom dance sequence is a powerful scene because it brings together the director's brilliant use of the camera and the characters.

An ALBERTO GRIMALDI Production
Marlon Brando
Last Tango in Paris
A Film by BERNARDO BERTOLUCCI
with MARIA SCHNEIDER · MARIA MICHI · GIOVANNA GALLETTI
and with JEAN-PIERRE LEAUD also starring MASSIMO GIROTTI
Produced by ALBERTO GRIMALDI Directed by BERNARDO BERTOLUCCI
A COPRODUCTION PEA PRODUZIONI EUROPEE ASSOCIATE S.A.S.—ROME LES PRODUCTIONS ARTISTES ASSOCIES S.A.—PARIS
X NO ONE UNDER 17 ADMITTED
United Artists Classics

As for people saying Brando was the best actor in the world, maybe. But he was also one of the most cantankerous and difficult of personalities who, I know on later films, caused huge headaches and even mental breakdowns.

LEACHMAN, CLORIS
Actress

Although our relationship lasted but a short time, my PR partner Richard Guttman and I were enlisted to plan an Oscar campaign for Cloris and her wonderful performance in *The Last Picture Show*, and it was great fun – for the most part.

Our first meeting took place at her Mandeville Canyon house. We arrived and continually rang her doorbell, to no avail. After a while we tried the door, found it was open and decided to enter. There was Cloris tinkling the ivories in the spacious living room and what's more, she was naked. Her opening line was: "Relax guys I will be with you in a minute" which turned out to be at least twenty.

Her robe rested on top of the piano and she carefully draped it around her shoulders and we started the brief discussion of our plans. She was happy with everything we proposed and was very pleased to undertake interviews with whomever we recommended.

After her nomination was announced she thanked us profusely and said that if she won she would thank us on the live broadcast, as we had been intrinsic to making it all happen. As we watched the show and heard the result – she had won – our thoughts of being praised reached a climax – no press agent, up to that time, had ever been acknowledged. Then came her acceptance speech in which she praised her first music teacher and everyone else … well, almost.

LEAN, DAVID SIR
Director, Producer

One of the perks of my job is getting acquainted with some of the giants of the movie world.

Sir David Lean arrived at a cable TV station, Z Channel, I was involved with to promote *A Passage to India*. I had the opportunity to keep

David Lean.

him company while the TV cameras were being set up, and when his car never arrived to escort him back to his hotel, he asked if I'd mind giving him a lift.

If he had only directed three motion pictures in his entire career then *Doctor Zhivago, The Bridge on the River Kwai,* and *Lawrence of Arabia* would have been enough to sustain his fame for all eternity.

David revealed much concerning his illustrious career that night, and one soon discovered that he was not completely satisfied with any of his films. He said that he could have always returned to the soundstage to make them better. There were certain scenes that he felt were good, but overall he thought the final result could always be improved upon. I should quickly add that he didn't dislike his films, or making them; there was no doubting that he was very much in love with the creative process – the joy of creating a celluloid dream had no comparison for him. It would be true to say that given infinite budgets and schedules, then David would be in his heaven. It was the producers, the money men, the clock watchers that he disliked. They – far from being the ones who financed his films – he saw as the ones who interfered!

"There are so many difficulties in making motion pictures as one has absolutely no idea how any of them will turn out," he espoused. "With a theatrical play, one rehearses and rehearses and rehearses until the combination of scenes work and one can see the whole entity with the run-through."

That statement gives one the impression that the director would have rehearsed for months given the time and money but, as we all know, the film business is just that – a business; it has to turn a profit to sustain itself.

He did, of course, have limited rehearsal time and used it wisely with the cast in working on scene interpretations, explanations of certain dialogue confrontations as he envisaged them, but also to relax the actors and for them to get to know one another. It was for these reasons that he rarely ever exceeded the third take of any scene.

Aside from producers, David also had contempt for the British unions. They didn't allow workers to mix their crafts and David was consequently resented for wearing the hats of a director, 3rd assistant director, editor and, at times, acting wardrobe mistress. He felt that this was the true path to knowing how movies were made – by experiencing the business at each and every level. The unions were minded otherwise and accused him of putting others out of work.

His approach to directing was analogous to an artist who understands how to mix paints, apply them to the canvas, and as such, create a picture to his satisfaction. Much preparation was given to how his "canvas" was to develop, in the form of storyboards. He was in fact one of the champions of storyboards – picturing the script, scene by scene – which actually arose through misunderstandings involving the written words of earlier screenplays. Nobody misunderstands a picture and therefore every one of the artists and crew were given copies.

In his on-screen discussion, David talked about some of his films, and I was particularly keen to discuss one of my personal favourites, *The Bridge On The River Kwai*.

Alec Guinness was so sure he would not win the Oscar after his nomination was announced, and in fact lost a sizeable bet to Lean. William Holden became a great friend of Lean who commented that Americans had, as a rule, greater discipline for film than their British counterparts, who are more theatrical by training. The theatre allows more freedom of expression whereas film, which is generally shot out of sequence, has to appear matchless.

I had always thought that the bridge was one of the great miniature models, and that combined with studio set-ups and projection techniques were how the industry craftsmen "fooled" the movie-going public. In this case I really goofed.

Lean thundered "My dear boy I will send you a photograph of my standing with producer Spiegel on the finished product, which cost $250,000 in 1956 and stood well over 400 feet tall at its highest. And one day I will tell you the problems with the script, which I basically wrote based on Pierre Boulle's book, and for which he got screenplay credit and the Oscar – and to think he could scarcely speak the language."

Lean was perhaps a little unfair with his statement about the script, as whilst they had all agreed on the rewrite to make it work, the reason Boulle was solely credited was because there were two other writers brought into the project who should have really been acknowledged – blacklisted Carl Foreman and Michael Wilson – who were denied eligibility to the Academy Awards because of their supposedly communist leanings. They were posthumously credited years later, in 1984, at a special Academy ceremony. (When the film was restored the names of Wilson and Foreman were added to the credits.)

David revealed the major disappointment of his life was in not being able to remake *Mutiny on the Bounty*, despite his spending more than five years on the project and building the two ships. He saw the studio executives as being interfering and that they wouldn't give him the budget he needed. In truth, it was a lot more complicated, as he wanted to split the script into two films, at twice the cost, and ended up falling out with Warner Bros. before taking it elsewhere where, again, he fell out and was forced off the project.

Lean was a prolific director, and at one time the biggest name in the business. Spielberg idolizes him and his work. While he worked less and less in his later years, he turned out fine movies such as *Ryan's Daughter* and *A Passage to India*, yet the money men were always cautious about backing him – fearing he was uncontrollable.

Passage to India was to be his final movie, as he died midway through trying to get *Nostromo* together. It was a terrific film to go out on though, and he said it was all conceived 25 years after visiting Oxford, where a stage version of the E.M. Forster book was produced. The author was so touched by the presentation that he gave half of the movie rights to the stage director, and as the years passed David became more and more intrigued about the idea of a film, and wrote the script. He cast his favorite actor Alec Guinness, Australian actress Judy Davis, and newcomer Victor Banerjee, and was sweating on his financing until two weeks before shooting started. With money tight David also edited the film, utilizing his past successes of being in the cutting room.

It was never easy for David though. *Lawrence Of Arabia*, he said, became a five-year struggle to get to the screen. It came about after Sam Spiegel developed an obsession with the life of Thomas Edward Lawrence, who saw action in World War I disguised as an Arab, and led the revolt against the German Army in Turkey. He thought Cary Grant would prove masterful casting, having seen the actor in the 1939 war epic *Gunga Din*. Grant turned it down though. Then came Albert Finney, who walked out after a few days, stating that he did not want to spend a year in the desert to become a movie star. Brando and Burton were considered but then Katharine Hepburn suggested Peter O'Toole, whom she had seen in the London theatrical version of *The Long and the Short and the Tall*. Spiegel and Lean agreed that the test was dynamite and it then took 18 months to get a script on which everyone could agree.

Lean's final comment on the film was that they had to transport water nearly 200 miles to their locations, and that was some feat!

In reflecting on trying to set up one of his other great epics, *Dr. Zhivago,* David said: "I made a trip to Moscow with the intention of finding suitable locations for the great Pasternak book and was rebuffed by the Russians at every turn. Sure, they wanted the revenues that this costly production would have engendered, but what resulted was my being made persona non grata, and subsequently we decided to use Finland as the alternative."

Tackling such a huge story was tricky. The narrative was so vast that it would have taken five movies. Writer Robert Bolt dissected the main scenes and decided that the characters would have to have new dialogue different from the book so that the story could flow from the diminished storyline.

Finland was used as a substitute for Russia and other scenes were filmed in Spain with some second-unit in Canada. Freddie Young, the cameraman, shot in 35mm, which was blown up to 70mm.

Maurice Jarre wrote Lara's theme after the film had been scored, when it was discovered that the authentic Russian theme they had used was still in copyright and could not be used!

David was a charming man and I feel privileged to have known him. I remember him saying that above all else he wanted to be thought of as a story teller. Not a bad epitaph.

LEMMON, JACK
Actor

In my (former) life as a journalist I got to know Jack, as he would always find time to talk, be it at restaurants or movie premieres, about projects he was working, which helped me fill some column inches. He was quite the raconteur too, and loved nothing better than to share a few stories; in particular about his idol and favorite actor, Marcello Mastroianni.

It was Billy Wilder, during the filming of *Some Like It Hot*, who introduced the pair in his office. At that time Mastroianni could speak very little English, and at the first meeting he kept saying "Scoootch" in his heavy Italian accent, and Jack wondered what he was saying. Only with hand gestures did Jack he recognize that he wanted a drink!

Five years later they met again in New York at a restaurant and again he shouted across a crowded room "Scoootch" which drew much

With the wonderful Jack Lemmon.

laughter from them both. Only in 1985 did the pair have the good fortune to work together, in Naples, on *Macaroni* when Jack portrayed a WWII veteran who returns years later and meets his Italian war buddy, who was the brother of his wartime lover.

Alas, the film wasn't very successful due to a weak script, but they had fun together.

Jack spent most of his career making comedies, but managed to breakout with his outstanding performance as the alcoholic in *Days of Wine and Roses*.

LIFE IS BEAUTIFUL
Feature film (1998)

When I first attended the Miramax screening of this little Italian film by Roberto Benigni I was transfixed.

His Chaplinesque character chose to prejudice his own life in a World War II concentration camp with his comedic take-off of a game that children played, which was quite brilliant. I marvelled at the sanitation of the daily life of the prisoners and couldn't quite take in the sheer atrocities that were the norm of their incarceration.

An idea struck me. Wouldn't this be a wonderful film for school teachers to show their pupils? It lacked the horrific sights that we saw in, say, *Schindler's List*, but at the same time it showed just how innocent people were imprisoned without cause. The horror may have been absent, but the unjustness and brutality of the regime was not.

At the previews there were a number of teachers present and agreed with my idea, so we set it up. The word of mouth created by students, we discovered, transmitted to the parents and a want to see film was thus created.

Academy members took the film to their hearts and not only voted it Best Foreign Language Film of 1998, but also nominated it in the Best Film category. The Oscar was awarded to the wonderful Roberto Benigni for his acting, as well as further nominations for direction and writing.

In one of the most memorable acceptances in recent memory, Benigni – genuinely surprised at his name being read out – climbed over the seats in the auditorium to reach the stage. It was a much-deserved win.

LITTLE VOICE
Feature film (1998)

Miramax, then run by Bob and Harvey Weinstein, had a knack of spotting low-budget hits.

British actor Jim Cartwright had written a play called *The Rise and Fall Of Little Voice* for his actress friend Jane Horrocks – who first captured the hearts of movie goers as a bespectacled anorexic in Mike Leigh's food-themed *Life Is Sweet* (1991) – to showcase her wonderful ability to mimic great singers such as Judy Garland, Shirley Bassey, Marilyn Monroe, Edith Piaf, and so on. It was a great hit.

A movie version was then set into being, and director Mark Herman worked on adapting the stage play.

Jane Horrocks was to star and Brenda Blethyn was cast as her mother.

My client, Michael Caine, at this time – by his own admission – was at a bit of a low ebb. He'd not made a feature film since *Blood and Wine* in 1996. "I made a few tv movies," he said "but nothing that came in excited me. I was just biding my time with the tv stuff…and hoping."

Then, one morning, a script landed on his desk. He called out to Shakira "this is it, this is it!"

He felt the slimy manager character of Ray Say was one of the best written parts he'd read in a long time. He didn't hesitate to accept. Both he and Jane won many great reviews along with Golden Globes and BAFTAS.

There was some doubt as to whether Jane actually sang the songs, or just mimed to the original recordings. Let me assure you, that was all Jane Horrocks!

LITTMAN, BOBBY
Agent

Bobby Littman was an agent and raconteur. He always wore Saville Row suits and a different collared boutonniere every day, and with his extreme example of British style would regale his friends and acquaintances with stories about the rich and famous of Hollywood. One such story is worth a spot just as it was told to me.

Bobby was the agent talent representing Gene Wilder, whose career in Hollywood from *The Producers* through *Young Frankenstein* and *Blazing Saddles* made him a hot property for the studios. Producer Dino De

Laurentis sent a script for Bobby to read on behalf of his star client. Recognizing that it was beneath the literary standard to which Wilder was accustomed he had to tactfully turn down the project, but at the same time avoid any unpleasantness so future offers would still be forthcoming. Bobby called Dino saying that his client was unavailable and that he would return the script post haste with apologies.

Two weeks later Bobby received a large envelope with the same script in. Somewhat bemused why Dino should be again forwarding the project, he read the attached letter, which after thanking him for his script submission, stated "this property does not fit into the De Laurentis current production schedule" and that they were therefore returning it.

Does the right arm know what the left arm is doing in Hollywood I ask?

LONGEST YARD, THE
Feature film (1974)

The Longest Yard is a 1974 football-prison story that was directed by my client Robert Aldrich, and scheduled its wrap party at Paramount with stars Burt Reynolds, Bernadette Peters, Eddie Albert, and Richard Kiel in attendance. The time came for the expected boring speeches thanking everyone from the stars and crew to the financiers, distributor, and even the teamsters.

Burt Reynolds, noted for his dry wit, was extolling the virtues of all and sundry when he was suddenly being heckled by his old friend Jack Cassidy – who'd obviously had too much to drink. This continued for a while until Burt could stand it no longer and screamed out "While you are making these inane remarks, Marty Ingels is sitting on your furniture."

This was a reference to the fact that Jack's wife, Shirley Jones, was having an affair with Marty Ingels. Needless to say, Jack suddenly sobered up and walked out of the event with this tail between his legs.

M

MACMURRAY, FRED
Actor

Born to Maleta Martin and Frederick MacMurray (a concert violinist), Fred MacMurray sang and played in orchestras to pay his way. After college he joined an orchestra in Hollywood where he was also able to supplement his income with a few extras roles, before eventually turning his hand to vaudeville – he played the circuits and night clubs until he managed to get some more movie acting jobs.

For a man who never studied acting, Fred astounded the Hollywood community by being able to boast that in all of his years in the business, he was never once unemployed.

Our paths crossed on many occasions when I was wearing my journalist's hat, and his wry recollections of his early start in nightclubs during prohibition made for great conversation. "Did you know I played saxophone with a group called Californian Collegians and on Broadway in *Roberta* (1933) with Bob Hope?" No I didn't!

Screen tested by Paramount in 1934, Fred was almost immediately selected for a series of odd roles, and by the following year had appeared in seven movies, including a loan out to RKO in *Alice Adams*. His first real friend at the studio was Carole Lombard, who gave him some sage advice. "Go to Palm Springs now that your contract renewal calls for only 250 dollars a week and lose yourself for a while."

Fred worried that he might be dismissed, but he went to Palm Springs and heard from his agent after a short while that a substantial raise was to be forthcoming. However, he had to agree to at least four motion pictures a year for the studio. In reminiscing with me about his 85 features, he recalled his first major role in *The Gilded Lily* opposite Claudette Colbert, he felt the pressure and kept blowing his lines. "It led to sleepless nights until she took me under her wing and secretly rehearsed with me, enabling me to overcome my fears."

Fred also told me that the stills department asked them to act out scenes from the film BEFORE production had commenced so they could use them for publicity purposes – I'd not realized that!

I discovered that Fred was quite an insecure man in his chosen career. "I turned downed Billy Wilder's offer of *Double Indemnity* you know." He told me. I asked why. "I didn't believe I had the ability to carry it off."

Thankfully, Wilder didn't take no for an answer and Fred was cast in the 1944 hit movie, now regarded as a classic of all time.

"I turned him down again too," Fred added "when he offered me *The Apartment* in 1960. It's a good thing Billy never took no as an answer from me, isn't it?"

MAN WITH ONE RED SHOE, THE
Feature film (1985)

This remake of a very funny French farce, *The Tall Blond Man with One Black Shoe*, starred Tom Hanks and was all about a CIA conspiracy to wrongly eliminate an innocent man. Sadly it lacked one element – comedy.

Despite having Tom Hanks and director Stan Dragoti, it didn't have a funny script and therefore there was no chance any of the terrific talent on board could raise any laughs.

I was asked to handle the release publicity and sell the film to the public.

Well, you can't sell an unfunny comedy, but you can hope to generate a bit of gimmicky publicity to try and get as many people into the theater in the first weekend as possible, before they realise it's not funny and word of mouth spreads, as the first weekend is always the most important to a movie. Fail and the movie sinks, get moderate success and it stands a chance of making some of its money back.

I arranged it so movie-goers were told in advance that they would only be allowed in to see the film on condition they wear one red shoe. The ensuing coverage we got was fantastic – much better than the film in fact! More than 400 people participated and I often wondered where same-sized feet movie-goers got together and shared one red pair of shoes?

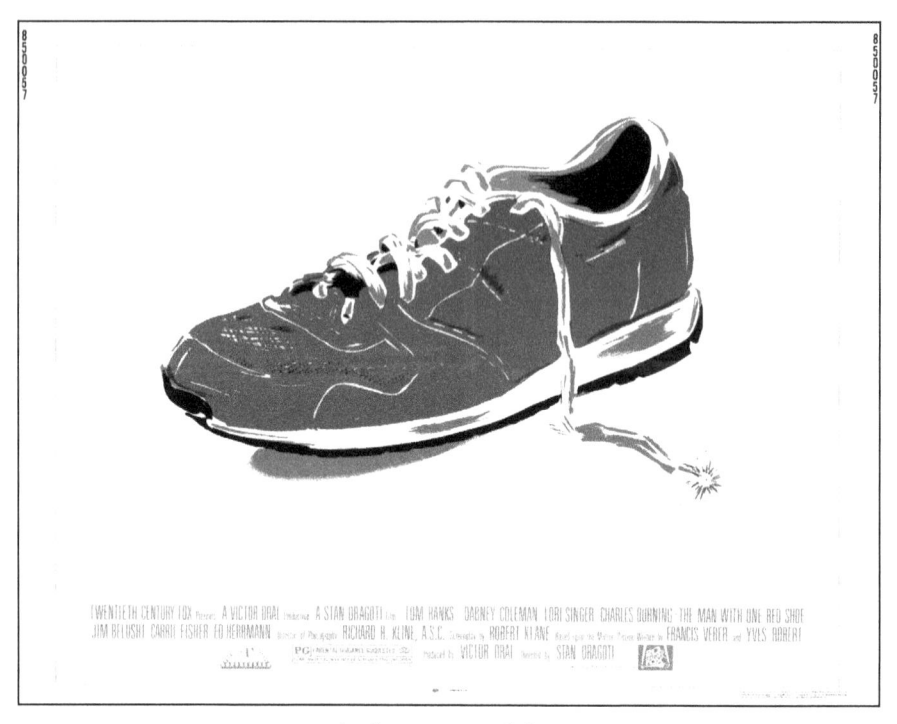

The famous one red shoe.

It debuted at no. 7 at the box office and over its opening weekend grossed $8,645,411 – about half its budget. It was all downhill from there though!

MARTY
Feature film (1955)

Hollywood publicist Walter Seltzer had been in charge of furthering the success of a major independent production company, Hecht-Lancaster, a partnership between Burt Lancaster and Harold Hecht. The (then) current film from their fold to be promoted – rather ironically given that Lancaster would never take part in publicity for films he starred in, but as a producer it was a different matter, as he expected his cast to tow the line – was a pretty low budget one, with a fairly unknown actor in the title role. Thus, I became involved with *Marty*, starring Ernest Borgnine.

"WONDERFUL!" ...Time
"A TRIUMPH!" ...Louella Parsons
"SUPERB, WARM, RICH!" ...Cue
"A FINE FILM...A GEM!" ...Life
"A SMASH!" ...Newsweek
"MARTY"
A HECHT-LANCASTER Production starring
ERNEST BORGNINE
and BETSY BLAIR
Story and Screenplay by PADDY CHAYEFSKY
Directed by DELBERT MANN · Produced by HAROLD HECHT
Associate Producer: Paddy Chayefsky · Released thru UNITED ARTISTS

Under Walter's excellent tutelage I planned an advertising and publicity campaign that took Hollywood by storm. Hal Tritel, a very talented illustrator, fashioned a line drawing of Borgnine sitting in a telephone booth, which became the theme of a series of advertisements placed by United Artists, the distributor, in *Daily Variety* and *Hollywood Reporter*.

The ads were tongue-in-cheek and amusing for the most part, and quite a departure from the usual staid quotes stating how wonderful the film and performances were. Here are two examples:

The first showed an army barracks with soldiers fast asleep, all dreaming lovely dreams illustrated via a series of balloons, like in comic strips. Most of them depicted beautifully clad pin-ups of such stars as Lana Turner and Ava Gardner. The "coup de resistance" was one private dreaming of Marty in the telephone booth.

The second advertisement showed a safari group moving through the African bush. A column of soldiers herded beasts of burden, which were transporting all the equipment. At the tail end followed a magnificent bull elephant lugging the famous telephone booth. Having established the telephone booth trademark, these and subsequent advertisements had no copy lines, as everyone in Hollywood already knew the movie they represented.

We also placed a series of ads in the *Los Angeles Times* and one which captivated readers most was:

"I HAVE SEEN MARTY 122 TIMES AND I STILL THINK THIS IS THE BEST MOVIE OF THE YEAR." This was signed by the projectionist at the Fine Arts Theatre in Beverly Hills.

Then Seltzer devised a unique full-page ad. He stuck a real envelope on a blank page and on the outside, where the address should have been written, were the words: "STRICTLY PRIVATE FOR GEORGE JESSEL."

To our surprise, 27 copies of the letter were actually sent to Jessel. Of course, the only contents of the envelope were a publicity release to promote *Marty*.

As we continued with the ads, Academy members embraced our unique approach and waited for more unusual approaches to the campaign. Those who could assemble 20 Academy members to their homes were sent a projectionist and a print of the film for those guests. These were the days before VCR's, of course. I really believe we were the first to create the "FOR YOUR CONSIDERATION" headings on campaign advertising, and introduced the home "screener" for members who couldn't get to a theatre.

Just for the record, the five nominations for Best Actor for l955 were:

Spencer Tracy for *Bad Day at Black Rock,*
Frank Sinatra for *The Man with the Golden Arm,*
James Dean for *East of Eden,*
James Cagney for *Love Me or Leave Me*
and…the winner, *Ernest Borgnine for Marty.*
The film also won best picture, director, and screenplay.

MARX, SAM
Producer, Writer, Executive

Sam Marx was a fascinating man. He was recommended to Louis B. Mayer by legendary producer Irving Thalberg, for a job at MGM in the early 1930s. The day he reported to the studio, Robert Harris – the studio's story editor – resigned. Thus, Sam was immediately sent to replace him.

His loyalty to Mayer was second to none. In his book, which he wrote about Mayer, he revealed that actor Conrad Nagel gave Mayer voice lessons so that he could not only address the stockholders of Loew's Inc, the owner of MGM, but also make radio appearances.

"Mayer was very tough on some writers," he told me, "who he felt ridiculed the movie business and they were soon out of the studio. And as for Dorothy Parker, she used to shout 'Get me out of here, I'm as sane as anyone!'"

"When we think TV has a quick product turnaround, you must remember that we used to buy a story and after three weeks of filming and editing, that film would be screening in New York a month later to those moviegoers hungry for entertainment."

One day Mayer entered Sam's office and told him that he was through with the story editing job. "I'm going to make you boss of the writers," he said, "you are now a producer and your first assignment is *Lassie Come Home.*" Sam also produced the first *Andy Hardy* film with Mickey Rooney.

Some years after retiring, Sam returned to the studio to check the vast inventory of produced and un-produced scripts, and discovered – after 40 years! – a novel called *The Tenth Man,* which had been written under contract by Graham Greene. *The Tenth Man* was soon turned into a film, starring Anthony Hopkins.

He once made a very interesting statement, which I think he had drummed into him by Louis B. Mayer. It was "What happens if you make films for specialized audiences and they don't show up?"

That's why Mayer decreed all MGM films should be for ALL audiences. A wise man.

MATTHAU, WALTER
Actor

Just thinking of Walter brings back many happy memories. Our first encounter in 1978 was most unusual.

He was starring with my client, Glenda Jackson, in *House Calls*, and the location was three houses down from mine in North Hollywood. I didn't have far to travel to work. As I approached his dressing room one day I was surprised to see several children lined up outside a Winnebago with its door wide open. I then heard Walter spelling out "accommodation." The assistant director told me that during rest periods between scenes children challenged him in a continuous "spelling bee."

The wonderful Walter Matthau.

On being introduced to him he smiled and enquired if I would like to join in the contest, being conducted against the strains of Mozart's "Marriage of Figaro" – one of his favourite classical pieces. Not quite what you'd expect!

A couple of years later Ronald Neame assigned me to *Hopscotch*. While on location in Munich, filming during the annual beer drinking festival, he revealed that he took the movie against his better judgment, and only because of Glenda being cast. He was less than enthusiastic about contributing to the German economy, having had an aversion to all things, including automobiles, from that country since the war.

His wisecracks wowed Glenda and the crew day after day and his mood was upbeat. It was at Matthau's suggestion that Ronnie Neame signed Glenda – Walter and she had a great chemistry in *House Calls* and they were very keen to work together again.

Having to write his biography for the press kit enabled me to get a rather comprehensive background of his theatrical start.

"Do you know I appeared in 18 plays on Broadway?" he told me, "and most of them were flops. Mind you, this allowed me to take on so many roles that I regarded it as a great success overall, as the theatre gave me so much valuable experience. Can you imagine if I'd had a hit and been in it for years? I'd never have learnt anything!"

He later notched up more than 100 TV appearances, in the likes of *Lux Video Theatre, Climax Theatre, Goodyear Televsion Playhouse, Robert Montgomery Presents*, and the like, though strangely never aspired to a movie career. He maintained that one had to be "pretty" to make it in movies, and with his hound dog looks, he stood no chance. However, when Burt Lancaster saw him in the New York staged play *Will Success Spoil Rock Hunter?* (1955) he was cast as a heavy in *The Kentuckian* (1955). That led to Kirk Douglas noticing him and casting him as a baddie in *The Indian Fighter* later that year.

With a movie career blossoming, Walter said that he regarded Hollywood "As a place that allowed me to make money so that I could return to the New York stage."

I asked him when he finally felt he'd "arrived" in Hollywood and a film career. He said it wasn't until eight years later in 1963 when he made *Charade* with Cary Grant. "They called me the Lithuanian Cary Grant," he quipped.

His comedic stardom was cemented with *The Fortune Cookie* and *The Odd Couple* – both of which he starred in opposite Jack Lemmon. From there, he never looked back.

Billy Wilder, who directed *The Fortune Cookie*, told me in an interview that he was a great fan of Walter's, and when the film almost fell apart halfway through when Walter suffered a heart attack, Wilder told United Artists (the backer), who were discussing replacing him, "If he is gone, so am I." They waited for Walter to recover. Happily, he won the Best Supporting Actor Oscar for his performance.

One of Walter's favorite films was *Cactus Flower* because, he said, "Here I was playing a dentist and the prim and proper nurse who fell in love with me was Ingrid Bergman. How fortunate could I be in life?"

They say that three's a charm, and for the thirdtime director Ronnie Neame selected Walter for a film – *First Monday in October*. He threw himself into the role and researched American law quite extensively.

Walter came over to me one day and asked "Do you know what the 12th Amendment states, Jerry?" I didn't. "Believe it or not, there cannot be a president and vice-president from the same state." He found it fascinating.

The film coincided with the first female judge being appointed to the court by President Reagan, though somehow Paramount Studios failed to capitalize on real and reel life coinciding.

Walter always said he would grow old disgracefully, and he certainly did with lovely films such as *Grumpy Old Men*. The last time I saw him was in 1995, in a Beverly Hills restaurant. He'd just finished *The Grass Harp*.

"Hey Jerry, have you learned to spell mellifluous yet?" he asked. He remembered I'd discovered the word when we were filming *Hopscotch* and I used it far too many times in everything I said and wrote – though frequently spelt it incorrectly! What a lovely man he was.

METEOR
Feature film (1979)

This multi-million dollar science fiction picture from Warner Bros. and American International Pictures was directed by my good friend Ronnie Neame. He was fresh from a great success with *The Poseidon Adventure*, and while this project had seen a number of wonderful illustrations and posters created, there was just one thing missing – a script!

A few months later that was taken care of and casting commenced: Sean Connery, Natalie Wood (as the production needed an actress who could speak fluent Russian – and she was born of Russian parents), Karl

Memoirs of a Hollywood Publicist • 163

Malden, and Martin Landau. Then Trevor Howard was cast too, in a three-day cameo as a British expert on meteors. On paper it looked good. It was anything but!

Locations included the Bavarian Alps for snow sequences, but there was no snow, so the unit moved to Chamonix. It was then obliged to take in Hong Kong (where some additional finance was secured for the budget via Run Run Shaw) and ended up back at Pinewood Studios.

The schedule overran with various problems – locations and effects delays, etc. – and it felt like it would never end. When principle photography eventually did reach the last day we had T-shirts made up saying "There Is Life after Meteor."

The budget spiralled in post-production. The ten-million-dollar movie saw another six million added to it in effects work, and not very satisfactory effects at that. The scary meteor was said to look more like Halley's Comet than a "five miles wide piece of rock travelling at 30,000 mph."

It was not a happy or successful experience for any involved.

I guess meteors just aren't that scary? It's one thing watching *Jaws* and thinking about swimming in the ocean again, but when sci-fi writer Isaac Asimov (whose article inspired the film initially) said in interviews "The chance of such a strike is very small, but not zero…the chance of a meteor hitting a populated center is very small, but not zero…" it didn't really stir the fear and anticipation hoped for by the producers!

MIRAMAX
Film studio

The things I learned from my various experiences with Oscar campaigning have carried me on to this day, and it has been my wonderful pleasure in becoming associated with Miramax for over fifteen years in an Oscar campaigning capacity.

The chance association came about through David (now Lord) Puttnam, who felt he owed me something because of the odd things I had accomplished for him through the years. He's another good guy. The telephone rang one day and the conversation went as follows:

"Is this Jerry Pam? My name is Harvey Weinstein and I received a call from David Puttnam who said that I was crazy if I did not hire you to do some work for Miramax."

Wow. I was somewhat dumbfounded – pleasantly so that is. After the proverbial 15 seconds of silence I was only able to convey my thanks and agreement.

In no time at all I was aboard, and I must confess it has been the most rewarding period of my professional life.

I have encountered every conceivable problem in this business and have found there is certainly a great negative force that pervades Hollywood – and it is based on ego, insecurity, and jealousy. The fact that Miramax has done so well, particularly with the Academy Awards each year, has raised the ire of many of the competing companies. What many fail to understand is quite simple; Miramax prides itself on relationships and values them. The staff under the direction of the Weinstein brothers, Harvey and Bob, all have a love of the movie art form that transgresses pure commercialism.

Some years back, Harvey and Bob realized there is a movie audience among the thinking public, and therefore a market for intelligent cinema – as well as the basic shoot-em-up and mindless action fare that caters for the lowest common denominator. Of course, the latter is the mainstay of the general stock-in-trade programmer, but that isn't to say it is – or has to be – the sole programming in theaters.

I can best summarize Miramax's success in this field by telling you about a short film they produced to highlight the first 25 years of the company's existence. There were clips of such films as *My Left Foot, Cinema Paradiso, Shakespeare in Love, Life is Beautiful, The English Patient, Il Postino, Chicago, The Cider House Rules, The Talented Mr Ripley, Good Will Hunting*, and *The Quiet American*, to name but a few. One can see their diversity and class that has made them so successful. I'm proud to be associated with them.

The Weinstein's operated Miramax with more creative and financial independence than any other division of Disney (who bought it in 1993), until September 30, 2005, when they decided to leave the company and founded The Weinstein Company. Miramax was sold by Disney to Filmyard Holdings, a joint venture of Colony Capital, Tutor-Saliba Corporation, and Qatar Investment Authority, in 2010, ending Disney's 17-year involvement with the studio.

MOORE, ROGER SIR
Actor, Director, Producer

Along with Howard Keel, one of the first people on my list to visit upon joining MGM was the dashing British actor.

We seemed to strike up a mutual affinity to one another right away. Over 50 years later we are still the best of friends and I continue to work on his behalf.

At that time, at MGM, the publicity machine was cranking up to build him as the screen's new romantic star in *Diane*, in which he appeared opposite Lana Turner. Roger was a relatively new signing to MGM, whose contract system was actually reaching the end of its life, and he confided that he was amazed to be in Hollywood, rubbing shoulders with the likes of Clark Gable, Walter Pidgeon, and Spencer Tracey – all of whom he'd idolized at the Odeon in Streatham, south London, much the same as I had.

Of all the stars I have met and represented, Roger Moore seems to be one of a few who is unchanged in attitude and disposition through the years.

Ever since I was assigned to Roger at MGM we seem to have had a bond – even before Bond. Maybe our stupid British sense of humour was the uniting force behind our friendship? Whatever, we continued through good and bad times while he toiled through costume films and undistinguished potboilers.

Here are Roger and I in our days at MGM.

After parting ways with MGM, he returned to England to shoot a TV series called *Ivanhoe,* and soon after that returned to LA with a contract at Warner Bros.

During this period, with TV in its infancy, Roger appeared in many Warner shows: the not so-good *The Alaskans*; the excellent *Maverick,* portraying cousin Beau; *77 Sunset Strip* and *The*

Roaring 20's were added to his resume; as were features *Gold Of The Seven Saints* and *The Sins Of Rachel Cade,* before obtaining his release from the studio.

When filming *The Alaskans,* by the way, there was a writers' strike and Roger wondered how he kept getting new scripts. In investigating, he discovered that they were scripts from *Maverick*, which just had the cast of characters name changed!

There was a general attitude at that period, regarding actors who appeared regularly on TV, that they could not resume appearances in movies due to a stigma that was attached to the small screen. There were a few exceptions with stars like Steve McQueen and James Garner, but the exceptions seemed to follow the rule. Roger had punctuated his TV work with features though, and from Warner's went to Italy to make a couple of epics – on which he met his third wife Luisa.

* * *

Back in London, in 1962, his agent received an offer from impresario Lew Grade to portray Simon Templar in a tv series of Leslie Charteris' bestselling novels of *The Saint*. The role was tailor-made for Roger, who spent the next seven years playing the dashing adventurer.

I flew to England to lend support, and to also gather publicity material for the American press. On arrival at Borehamwood Studios for the initial filming, Roger told me about the Volvo P1800 car, which Simon Templar would make famous the world over. The producers had originally wanted the very popular Jaguar XK 120. They contacted Jaguar about a deal but the car manufacturer told the producers that there was an 18-month waiting list, and the company therefore felt that they did not need any further exposure for the model. The request was turned down – that is, unless the production wished to buy one – and wait! What a difference in America where a producer could have several automobiles without cost just for the sheer promotion.

They next approached Volvo, who couldn't do enough to help. Two models were put at the company's disposal and Roger bought one of them and used it as his own personal car – which he drove to and from the studio.

With the gigantic success of the series in Britain, Lew Grade was more than disappointed when the American TV networks turned down the series. He was forced to syndicate the show. No show had ever made the switch from syndication to network prime time, but such was *The Saint*'s success that two years later NBC had second thoughts and acquired all rights. That's when they moved into filming in color.

It was during this period that Roger became interested in directing – and had his union ticket from a previous short-lived career as an animator – and was subsequently assigned some shows to helm. When one of the two producers, Monty Berman, decided to leave the series and make other shows; the remaining producer, Bob Baker, asked Roger to join him in his company. Thus, Roger became star, director, and producer of the show.

For the seven years the show was in production the cast and crew were treated to Roger's humorous stories, anecdotes, and practical jokes. Working for such a period on a series could have been monotonous, but it certainly wasn't with Roger around!

Following 118 episodes, in 1969 Roger hung up his halo and announced plans to return to the silver screen in a series of movies. He produced *Crossplot* with his partner Bob Baker, and took the lead role, before EMI approached him with a project. *The Man Who Haunted Himself* provided moviegoers with a tense drama in which Roger played two roles – that of Harold Pelham, and that of his doppelganger. He turned in one of his finest screen performances ever, and the reviews were terrific!

Roger Moore has established himself as a hugely successful tv actor and was now destined for great things on the silver screen once again.

However, TV came knocking again. Lew Grade pitched Roger an idea for a series about a British aristocrat and a tough New Yorker, united in the fight against crime. It was called *The Persuaders*. Roger declined, but Lew was insistent – "I've already sold it with you and Tony Curtis in the leads," he said, "think of your queen, think of your country – it needs the income." He offered a generous pay check – how could Roger refuse?

In the event, Roger would only commit to one series of the show, as there was another role he was vying for.

When Sean Connery finally decided to quit as 007 saying "never again" after returning for one film following George Lazenby's brief time in the role, rumours in the press started about "the next Bond."

Roger was offered the part.

Guy Hamilton, the director of the next film in the series, *Live and Let Die*, was most pleased with the casting. He and Roger made a conscious decision to avoid any similarity to Sean's Bond – for instance, Roger never ordered a vodka martini, shaken nor stirred.

On location with Roger during his first Bond film.

On being invited to New Orleans for the bayou location of *Live and Let Die*, I was surprised to see Roger not only pounds lighter, but sporting a very short haircut. Gone were his long locks from *The Persuaders*. During the lunch break Roger hoisted me onto his new cabin cruiser and we sped out to Lake Ponchetrain. In attempting a return to the company's base, after whizzing up and down the numerous bayous, we realized that we were hopelessly lost.

Hoping to come across any signs of life, we encountered a sheriff after ages of searching, who was fast asleep in, of all things, a rowing boat. You can imagine his shock at being awakened by two men, one of whom was James Bond. In no time at all, he came aboard and guided us back to the location.

Being ninety minutes late to filming, we arrived back somewhat anxious, to discover that Guy Hamilton had sent out a search party! I was later asked if I had been worried about being lost in the wilds of Louisiana. "Scared? No way! I was with James Bond."

I remember another location I visited was on *The Spy Who Loved Me* (1977). Roger felt that the producers had all the right ingredients with this one – great story, lavish production values, good cast and fun, with director Lewis Gilbert.

I recall, located in Luxor, Egypt, the government-appointed censor was continually on the set making sure that there were no changes to the approved script. However, in the scene where Roger fights with steel-toothed villain, Jaws, who swings at a piece of scaffolding and demolishes the ruins they are fighting in, Roger had an idea for an ad-lib but wary of the censor, he just mouthed a line.

The sound man said "Sorry Rog, I didn't get that."

Roger told him not to worry, as they could do it in post-sync. The line was, of course, "Egyptian builders!"

Everyone had a great time.

For seven features, Roger played it in his own inimitable style – acting in a humorous light-hearted way. It endeared him to audiences around the world. He was a superstar in every respect of the word.

When Pierce Brosnan took over the mantle, Roger advised him to "Do it your way. I never set out to be different from Sean Connery, it just took a turn."

Jackie Collins, a close friend, commented that Sean acted as a "bad boy womanizer" whereas Roger "married the heroine." Michael Caine, Roger's closest friend, meanwhile said that "Sean machoed them into bed whereas Roger laughed them into it."

As I have said earlier, fame has in no way changed Roger's attitude at all. He is gracious at all times, always signs autographs, and wherever he travels his fans regard him as a long-time friend.

Post Bond he has entered a very important period of his life in becoming an ambassador for UNICEF (United Nations International Children's Emergency Fund). He has travelled to South America, the Far East, Asia, Africa, and all over Europe, raising funds and awareness for the charity. He is often called upon to speak at functions and fundraisers and this work, above any other, which he carries out with his

From Russia With Love! Roger and I freezing our butts off behind the old iron curtain.

fourth wife Kristina at his side, has made him happier than one could ever imagine.

He still enjoys acting though – when time allows. A decade or so back we visited Russia, twice in the same year, for David MacKenzie (the head of Associated Television International). He directed two TV specials revealing secrets of the infamous KGB, which Roger hosted. We were wined and dined in Moscow and St. Petersburg by dignitaries who had suddenly become aware of Roger's Bond films – which had of course been suppressed for over 25 years behind the Iron Curtain. They all knew him!

Often the first to denigrate his own talents, Roger does have an excellent philosophy on acting: "If the acting shows, then there is something wrong with it."

There is nothing wrong with his!

MOUSE ON THE MOON, THE
Feature film (1963)

Director Richard Lester was signed to direct this political satire upon being recommended to producer Walter Shenson by Peter Sellers (who had starred in *The Mouse That Roared* for Shenson a few years earlier), as Lester and Sellers had previously worked together on *The Goon Show*.

Shenson sent Lester the script and invited him to lunch at Pinewood Studios. They agreed to a deal and Shenson said "Let me show you our sets." Shenson led Lester to the backlot where Cornel Wilde's sets for *Lancelot and Guinevere* were still standing. "Here they are!" he said. Even though they were of a totally different period, Shenson had done a deal to buy the sets in order to save his production money!

The quirky little film did very well in Britain, though it's entirely British comedy cast weren't that well known in the States, and it didn't fare particularly well; but Walter had made his money back and that made it a big success by his standards!

MURDER ON THE ORIENT EXPRESS
Feature film (1974)

I was absolutely thrilled when Nat Cohen of E.M.I.- the British film distributor – called me and said his company wanted a campaign for *Murder on the Orient Express*. Furthermore, he explained, there should be particular emphasis placed on Ingrid Bergman's performance along with the star of the film, Albert Finney. Nat was very concerned that Finney's makeup, as the noted Belgian detective Hercule Poirot, was so perfect that few would recognize him. My campaign duly commenced with a photo from the film and the caption

"DO YOU KNOW THIS ACTOR?"

This was followed with a photo of Finney out of makeup.

It was certainly a terrific performance and very worthy of the Oscar nomination which did come his way. Mind you, Albert has always shunned awards and ceremonies, which of course he has every right to do, as it his belief that his work says everything he has to say. In the event, he didn't win, but the nomination alone saw offers flood in for other projects.

Ingrid Bergman was being pushed forward for the Best Supporting Actress category. However, she was concerned that her role in the film

Memoirs of a Hollywood Publicist • 173

was "insignificant" among the flock of the very talented and high profile supporting players – including Maggie Smith, Lauren Bacall, Jacqueline Bisset, Wendy Hiller, and Vanessa Redgrave.

I arranged for mass screenings in Hollywood and the Oscar voters clearly loved the nervous Swedish missionary she played, as they nominated her for what was her third Academy Award.

On Oscar night Ingrid insisted that I accompany her to the ceremony. To her great delight – and genuine surprise – she was named the winner in the category. She honestly could not believe it. After she came back to her seat in the audience, holding her Oscar tightly, she handed me the envelope containing the result of the balloting and said "You deserve this."

To this day I have this framed together with a photo taken at the event, with the caption:

"THE WINNER IS: INGRID BERGMAN IN "MURDER ON THE ORIENT EXPRESS."

On the back of the envelope were the words SUPPORTING ACTRESS printed above a red seal. It was night I will never forget.

N

NEAME, RONALD
Director, Producer, Cinematographer

You've probably seen his name mentioned many times already within these pages, and to be honest, if ever there was a greater character in filmdom I don't know who it could be. Right up until his death at the age of 99, Ronnie had a mind that is sharper than most 30-year-olds. His start in films was in the silent days with Alfred Hitchcock, loading cameras and rising through the ranks as a cameraman, producer, writer, and finally director.

One of Ronnie Neame's finest films, and the film on which we first met.

175

I first became involved with Ronnie when I was arranging the release publicity for *Tunes of Glory* in 1960. That was in the old days when we didn't very often have special invitations printed up for previews, so I wrote a letter inviting the various members of the press to a screening with an RSVP. On the letter, I affixed, by means of a stamp hinge, a British postage stamp of the coronation of King George VI and Queen Elizabeth – as something to grab their attention. When the invitees presented their invitations at the screening I discovered only 7 stamps still affixed – the press were not adverse to making a few bucks it seemed!

Roll on six years and I met Ronnie again while working on Michael Caine's first Hollywood feature, *Gambit*, and subsequently on *Hopscotch* and *Meteor*. Ronnie is a very calm, easy going director. He has a great knowledge of all aspects of production on the floor, having served in many of the roles, and was a great favorite of actors.

Ronnie finally secured what he called his "fuck you fund" through directing the classic disaster movie *The Poseidon Adventure* in the 1970s. It made an absolute fortune, enabling Ronnie to speak his mind to studios and would-be employers about what he really thought of future offers and scripts.

He had a very dry sense of humor too, and having been invited to address a luncheon of movie big-wigs in London, who were all keen to hear about his adventures on classics such as *Brief Encounter, In Which We Serve*, and *Poseidon*, he apologized for not having prepared anything and thought he would therefore speak about his new appointment as chairman of CRAFT. There were puzzled looks exchanged across the room as Ronnie spelled it out, "C-R-A-F-T, have you heard of it? It's a prestigious organisation open to people of advanced age." People shook their heads wondering if the famed director had perhaps missed the point of the talk – his life and times in movies.

Ronnie smiled and said, "Come on, C-R-A-F-T ... Can't Remember A Fucking Thing ... now, let me tell you about *The Poseidon Adventure* ..." and had everyone in the palm of his hands.

NEGULESCO, JEAN
Director

This French-sounding named director was in fact Romanian and lived opposite Johnny Green, who headed up MGM's music department for many years. We first met at a soiree at the Greens' house and an invitation followed to Jean's mansion, which I discovered had been built for Greta Garbo. Jean was a very talented artist and his home housed many of his terrific works together with oils and watercolors from the Art Deco period.

Jean had lived in Paris in the 1920s and won the Brancusi prize at the age of 25. Critics considered him a genius, and his figure-drawing became world famous. He also discovered up-and-coming talent, in particular Bernard Buffet. He had a keen eye for what he liked!

That such a talented artist and film-maker should also be a culinary master fascinated me – and his sumptuous dinners attracted a who's who of Hollywood.

In 1968 I was in Teheran working on *The Invincible Six*, which Jean directed, with Stuart Whitman, Elke Sommer, and Curt Jurgens starring. Jean said there was a part still to be cast – that of a corpse. He asked me to do it. I suggested he should ask Elke's husband, a *New York Herald Tribune* reporter, so I could observe how a great journalist plays it dead! So Jean asked and it made a great story in the *Tribune* – nicely plugging the film, of course.

Jean's career was very much up and down, as whilst he'd made many successful films for the studios' own productions over the years, he didn't always find it easy to get funding for his own projects, which were less financially commercial, but all the same worthy films. Hollywood was less interested in "worthy" than it was "dollars." Rather than continue suffering the frustration of arguing against the doubters, he made the brave decision to step back from the business after his 1970 film, *Hello-Goodbye*, to concentrate on art and writing. In his final few years he wrote his memoirs, entitled *Things I Did and Things I Think I Did*, which he illustrated throughout with line drawings.

He has a star on the Hollywood Walk of Fame at 6200 Hollywood Blvd.

O

OMEN, THE
Feature film (1976)

There are some scripts that, when you read them, make the hairs on the back of your neck stand up. This was one of those.

Undoubtedly, *The Omen* is one of the best horror films ever made.

A high ranking American diplomat, Robert Thorn, is told the child his wife was carrying died at birth. However, at that same time, a child was born to another woman in the same hospital. Tragically, that mother died during the birth and it is agreed that this orphaned baby should be said to be the son of Robert and Katherine Thorn, and that Katherine should never know any different…until he is discovered to be the antichrist, that is.

It was directed by Richard Donner, who at that time was more well known for helming classic U.S. tv shows – *Cannon*, *The Streets Of San Francisco*, *The Man From UNCLE*, *The Six Million Dollar Man*, *Petrocelli*, and *Kojak*. This was his first major movie – after it had first been offered to Mike Hodges, who turned it down.

Charlton Heston, Roy Scheider, and William Holden had all turned down the lead role and the film's star was now Gregory Peck, of whom I was a great admirer. So keen was he on the script that, to make the film, he took a huge cut in salary (his fee was $250,000) but was guaranteed 10% of the film's box office gross. When it went on to gross more than $60 million in the U.S. alone, *The Omen* became the highest-paid performance of Peck's career.

Everyone had heard of Peck, of course, and his most famous movies – *Captain Horatio Hornblower RN*, *Roman Holiday*, *Moby Dick*, *The Guns of Navarone*, *To Kill A Mockingbird*, and *Arabesque*, but they were some years earlier and he hadn't had a hit in some time. He wasn't a (currently) bankable name in terms of carrying a movie. One, rather cruel

Memoirs of a Hollywood Publicist • 179

studio executive said "Peck couldn't even get arrested here" – such was his low profile in Hollywood's eyes.

He wasn't known as a star of horror movies either, which gave me an interesting predicament. I felt that if I concentrated my efforts on Peck, then, with the greatest of respect, it would probably missell the movie. After much consultation with the director and studio, I decided to center my campaign on the mark of the anti-Christ: "666." I felt it was a very powerful and frightening image.

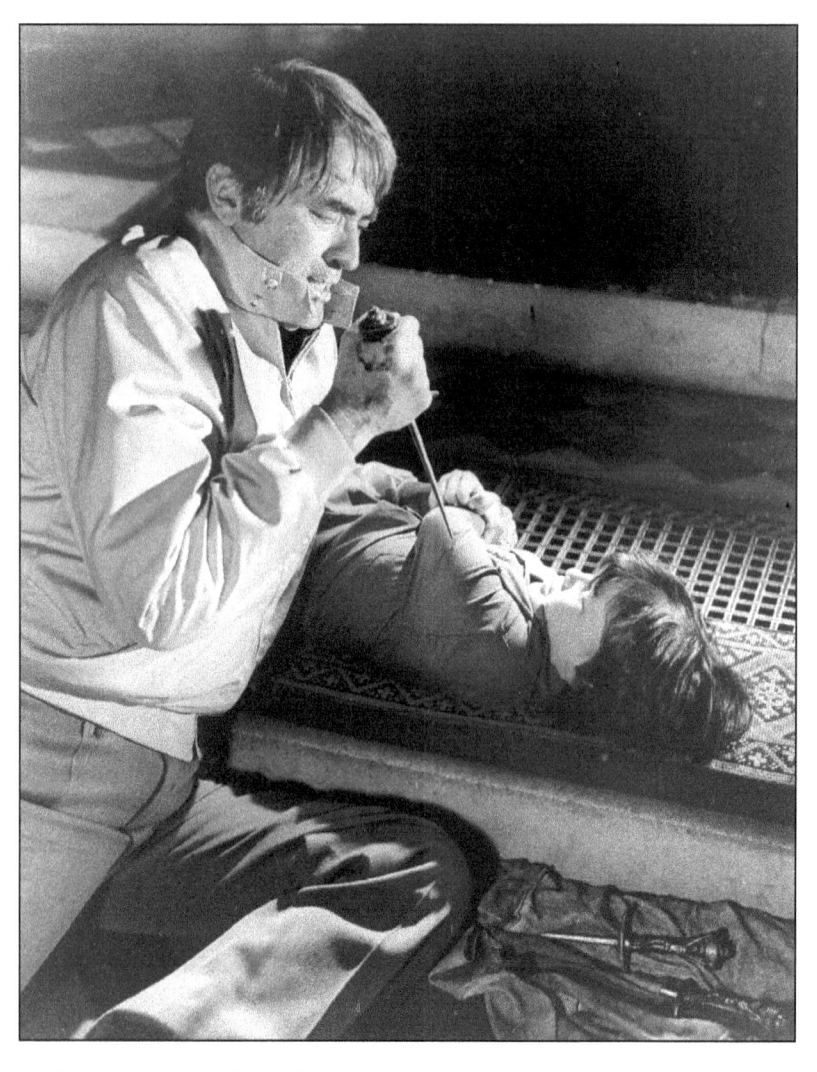

The climax to the chilling film, as Gregory Peck's character Ambassador Thorn, tries to kill Damien.

As part of my pre-release publicity campaign, and to point out the significance of "the three sixes" as "The Sign of Satan," I had the movie sneak-previewed nationwide in the USA on June 6, 1976 – 06/06/6.

While viewers in the theatres were busily being scared witless, we ensured that theater employees were out front putting up specially made posters declaring: "Today is the SIXTH day of the SIXTH month of Nineteen-Seventy-SIX!" Many a theatre patron literally freaked out upon seeing those posters as they left!

Of course, many remember the music as being one of the most frightening elements of the movie. It nearly never was though. Richard Donner and Harvey Bernhard asked Fox studio head Alan Ladd Jr. for extra money during the film's post-production period to hire composer Jerry Goldsmith, whose music they strongly felt was right for the movie. Ladd was dubious and suggested they hire a less expensive composer. After much cajoling Ladd finally agreed to hire Goldsmith. The composer delivered his first and only Academy Award win for his score.

The production, having earlier changed its title from *The Antichrist* to *The Birthmark*, was not without its troubles. In fact, some say that it was cursed!

Gregory Peck and screenwriter David Seltzer took separate planes to the UK from the States, yet BOTH planes were struck by lightning. While producer Harvey Bernard was in Rome lightning just missed him. Rottweilers hired for the film attacked their trainers.

A hotel at which director Richard Donner was staying got bombed by the IRA, and he was also struck by a car.

After Peck cancelled a flight to Israel, the plane he would have chartered crashed, killing all on board.

On day one of the shoot several principal members of the crew survived a head-on car crash.

Perhaps a higher power was trying to tell us something?

The film's haunting closing scene was all-important to Donner. He wanted to leave the viewers on the edge of their seats, and used reverse psychology on young Harvey Stephens, who played Damien – the antichrist – Thorne.

"Don't you dare laugh. If you laugh, I won't be your friend," he told the boy. Naturally, Stephens wanted to laugh, but instead smiled directly into the camera. It sent a shiver down my spine.

OSCAR CAMPAIGNS

I write a lot about Oscar campaigning, which to be honest is much the same as political campaigning. A publicist is hired for a film, actor, director, writer, or one of the film crafts, to create an awareness of his or her talent on the respective motion picture. It is the duty of the publicist to acquaint, or in some cases reacquaint, the members of the Academy of Motion Picture Arts and Sciences of the reasons that person is deserving of an Oscar nomination, or award. Politicians take advertisements to get elected, and much the same takes place in Hollywood.

My first entry into the world of Oscar campaigning took place in 1955 thanks to my good friend Walter Seltzer, who at that time was Hollywood's preeminent publicist, and asked I help him with an assignment. His happy demeanour, in spite of the rigors of having worked for many years at MGM and Warner's, was most infectious to everyone he came in contact with, and after being introduced to him by a mutual friend, my life changed for the better in more ways than one.

His philosophy was quite simple. "Show business is a game in which one should never take any situation seriously, because it is based on maneuvering people and situations into the right slots." I soon found out the accuracy of that statement.

P

PUTTNAM, DAVID LORD
Film producer

David Puttnam was once hailed as the savior of the British Film Industry. From carving a successful career in advertising and commercial, he entered the film production arena in the early 1970s and never looked back. He's been a good friend of mine for many years, really going back to his film *The Mission*, in 1986. His producing partner, Fernando Ghia, hired me to put together an Oscar campaign, and so our friendship was formed.

The Mission garnered six Oscar nominations, and won one statuette for the brilliant cinematography.

I had, a few years earlier, represented *Midnight Express* at the Cannes Film Festival, which he had produced, but I had dealt exclusively with the executive producer, Peter Guber.

David had achieved great success with hits such as *Chariots of Fire*, *The Killing Fields*, and *Local Hero*, and I think *The Mission* – while credited with bringing

Lord David Puttnam.

Goldcrest, the British company that funded it, to its knees with production problems and budget overspends (often beyond the production's control) – brought him to the attention of the studio bosses at Columbia as a potential president. David was offered the post. He was the first British person ever to be appointed to run a Hollywood Studio. As with any executive post one takes over, you inherit a certain amount of "in the works" projects. One such film was *Ishtar*. It was already shooting when David took over, and once he read the script he was horrified that it should have been green lit, with Dustin Hoffman and Warren Beatty no less. David refused even to screen the $40-million-dollar boondoggle, despite his company being responsible for its promotion and release.

David arrived in Hollywood with many noble intentions and plans. He was determined to smash the star system that was beginning to throttle the industry, and liberate the studio from its dependence on occasional blockbusters, by hiring talented young directors and writers to make lots of low-budget movies. Under his direction, Columbia was going to reinvent itself as a new creative force.

"Things," he told his staff, "are going to be different round here from now on." And things *were* different. At Christmas he gave the studio's entire Christmas gift allocation to charity, writing a memo to employees saying "enjoy a very happy Christmas knowing that your generosity has made it possible for many less privileged to feel cared for at this very special time of year."

He avoided the trap of big-budget production, remakes, agent-producer cronyism, and numerically designated sequels.

David and I often spoke, though he never employed my services – thankfully! He said "Jerry, I could give you any one of a list of films, but those in the publicity department in this studio would kill you. They'd be terrified that you were involved in a movie and would see you as encroaching on their territory, and a threat to their livelihood. You're too good a friend to lose." However, a few years later he did recommend me to Harvey Weinstein at Miramax, with whom I have enjoyed a terrific working association.

Puttnam in Hollywood wasn't to last though. There was no way that a Brit could launch what was seen as a "frontal attack" on the business and survive. Hollywood resented his candor (though many respected he was right) and one newspaper interpreted it as "priggish self-righteousness." "Death wish is a phrase that comes to mind as one reviews Puttnam's brief hour at Burbank." wrote Bernard F. Dick, a historian of Columbia Pictures.

David was eventually shafted in a corporate putsch, collected three million bucks in compensation, and returned to Britain a sadder, wiser, and richer man. The whole thing took just over a year from glorious start to sordid finish. Columbia, meanwhile, claimed that every film he green lit lost money. That is, of course, according to their accountancy practices.

David returned home and continued as an independent producer until 1999, when he stepped back from the film business (though has recently returned) to concentrate on political issues, in particular, education. He became President of UNICEF UK and remains one of the few members of the film producing community to be honored by Queen Elizabeth II, a total of three times. First he was made a Commander Of The British Empire (CBE) in 1982. In 1995 he was knighted, to become Sir David, and two years later was made a life peer with the title Lord Puttnam of Queensgate.

Q

QUIET AMERICAN, THE
Feature film (2002)

"The depth, breath, and distance from me made the character of Fowler in *The Quiet American* so perfect. Whenever I play a role that is the complete antithesis to me I get enthused and I believe this is my best performance as an actor, because I really am not there."

So said Michael Caine on the film, for which he was Oscar nominated as Best Actor.

It was of course a remake of the 1958 film and co-starred Brendan Fraser with Caine.

Michael Caine and Brendon Fraser in *The Quiet American*.

"*The Quiet American* is a massive lead for a guy of my age," he continued. "It's a great love story and a great spy story. And at 69, I got the girl! And it wasn't a 68-year-old girl either."

The film arrived on screens at the time of the 9/11 tragedy and created a terrible quandary as to how we might promote it. No matter how good a film or performances are, there are always external factors completely out of our control, and this was one of those occasions.

To put it simply, bad timing meant it didn't do very well at the box office, with the U.S. still feeling shaken by the terrorist attacks. With George Bush then announcing a "War On Terror," it seemed the last thing they wanted was a story of Vietnam – a war they lost.

Sadly, Michael didn't win the Oscar on this occasion, but I've a feeling we'd be hearing more from him soon!

R

RESTAURANTS

Of course, man cannot live by wine alone, and in Hollywood one learns fairly quickly that much business takes place in restaurants; and there are several that have made their mark in the film industry. I feel I should mention some of them as they were very much a part of Hollywood. Sadly, not all remain.

Ma Maison

Established by Patrick Terrail, a suave Frenchman and the nephew of Claude Terrail, owner of the famous Tour D'Argent in Paris, the restaurant was noted for its pressed duck; and for giving patrons, with their check, a number signifying how many ducks have been cooked since the succulent gastronomic entrée was introduced.

Unfortunately the Hollywood dining spot lacked much of the glitter and exotic background of its poor French cousin, but the food was most enjoyable and much of its success was due to noted Chef Wolfgang Puck, who subsequently left to form his own eatery, Spago, due to not being offered a partnership in Ma Maison, which he materially helped make famous.

As the famous line from *Casablanca* stated "Everyone dines at Rick's" and so it was with Ma Maison on Melrose Avenue. The tent like exterior was surrounded with Astroturf — the funkiness seemed to create the kind of atmosphere that show business embraced. Stars, agents, managers, lawyers, would-be starlets, and members of the press all frequented this American version of a bistro and, believe it or not, there was a snobiness that people talked about. The telephone number was unlisted and out front the very small parking lot was the scene of Rolls', Bentleys, and other exotic cars.

There were many regulars, including Orson Welles.

The expression "Thank God It's Friday" certainly applied to Ma Maison. This was the day that anyone who was anyone booked a table. As I had helped Patrick Terrail in the restaurant's early stages by taking many of my star clients there, he rewarded me by offering me table 2 any Friday I wanted it. Table 1 was normally taken by Hollywood lawyer Greg Bautzer, who had represented Howard Hughes in his heyday, and was later the legal counsel for Kirk Kerkorian, the big cheese at MGM Studios; along with many major stars in filmdom.

Robin Leach, who was a journalist before achieving fame on TV with his *Lifestyles of the Rich and Famous* program, was a regular and often had a crew there recording with subjects for the show. There was always a glitzy atmosphere.

It was certainly never dull, and along with the glamour there were a few not so glamorous incidents – such as when one Friday producer Sidney Beckerman slugged Hollywood agent Bobby Littman, breaking his nose in a fight that was seemingly about an old family feud, over which they'd been arguing all through lunch.

An amusing moment came when I was with Michael Caine one day. He was perusing the menu as the waiter approached and (thinking himself a smart ass) started talking in French about the specials of the day. Michael listened and didn't react in any way. When the waiter finished, Michael leant over and replied to him at great length in French – he was fluent in the language. The waiter stopped him by saying "Sir, I'm sorry but I only speak food in French!"

A native of Austria, Chef Wolfgang Puck became known for his creative menus and introduced what was to become a famed "Jewish pizza," which comprised smoked salmon and cream cheese on a pizza style base.

Patrick Terrail was certainly a showman; he loved Hollywood and its eccentricities. I remember one day hearing a poker playing group there send out for hamburgers to McDonald's, saying they were fed up with French food. Patrick, far from being angry, joined them in a burger and said he rather enjoyed the change of fare! He always walked around in clogs and people thought he was perhaps a little eccentric. "Ah no," he would say, "the public just don't realize that I am on my feet for many, many hours without ever sitting down and this is by far the most comfortable way for me to be so."

When he decided to sell the entire property a wonderful part of Hollywood disappeared forever.

Le Dome

Situated on Sunset Strip, Eddie Kerkhofs, the owner, embraced all segments of society. With its patio, which was created when the new no smoking rules came into being, and interior dining rooms consisting of banquettes and large and small tables, parties were a nightly scene celebrating everything from engagements, first nights and premieres, to wine clubs.

The success, apart from the various varieties of French and American food, was due to its owner who was always there greeting his guests and making sure that the seating was arranged to inspire a mutual togetherness, even though many of the patrons were not regulars.

They say that all good things come to an end, and it is with regret that I recall the day Eddie took a partner who sadly did not create the anticipated excitement of a new venture. Thus, Eddie left and has now established a new watering hole rejoicing in the name of Il Piccolino.

Chasens

This legendary restaurant saw more stars than in the heavens. Headed by Maud, widow of the late Dave Chasen, her clientele included presidents as well as the A to Z list of movie stars and directors, including Alfred Hitchcock, Billy Wilder, Cecil B. DeMille, Irene Dunne, Jack Benny, and so many more.

My first dinner was somewhat embarrassing as I had taken a major reporter there and had no idea that at that time they did not accept credit cards. I was saved from complete humiliation by borrowing some money from an actor client, who just happened to be at the bar waiting for his guests.

Above the bar was a model airplane of a TWA Constellation which was reportedly presented to the proprietors by the TWA owner, Howard Hughes.

Alas this, as with so many other wonderful establishments like Perinos, the Windsor, Tail of the Cock, and even the Cock and Bull are now gone and forgotten, except for the older crowd who used to frequent them.

ROYAL DINNER

With the announcement that the 1984 Olympic Games would be held in Los Angeles, it became incumbent on the 2.3 million British people resident in the U.S. to assist in the raising of funds to field as powerful an Olympic team as possible to come to America.

Thus, the British Olympic Association (USA) was formed in 1982. It existed to "provide a spirit of unity" and at the same time provide transportation for the British team.

At the center of the fundraising was a plan to develop a gala dinner. It was to be held at the Beverly Wilshire Hotel as part of an (non-televised) entertainment gala featuring British artists who gave their time and services for free.

HRH Prince Andrew meets the committee.

Michael Caine offered to head the entertainment committee and a meeting was called to discuss the structure of the show, with Sir Gordon White agreeing to become the chief sponsor, and Leslie Bricusse, Tony Adams, and Caine acting as producers. I became associate producer and it was my responsibility to handle the logistics as well as the schedules for rehearsals, etc.

Many meetings later, on April 8, 1984, a lavish cocktail party was thrown to precede our gala dinner, with HRH Prince Andrew attending as guest of honor, along with his wife Sarah (aka Fergie). Those attending had paid either $500 or $1,000 per plate, and everyone was introduced to the prince and had a photograph with him.

Lord Lew Grade, the British TV impresario and producer of top shows such as *The Saint* and *The Muppets*, as well as movies *On Golden Pond, Sophie's Choice*, and a *Pink Panther*, was the honorary dinner chairman, and with great pride announced every seat had sold out.

Michael Caine and Roger Moore together introduced the cast of Julie Andrews, Tony Newley, Dudley Moore, Cary Grant, Tom Jones, Cleo Laine, Johnny Dankworth, Michael York, and Sheena Easton. The Jack Elliot orchestra provided the music, and we danced the night away until 1:15am.

One of the highlights of the night was the auctioning of a David Hockney painting, purchased by Michael York's wife, Pat, for $45,000, and a set of caricatures of the night's entertainers was sold to agent Lew Wasserman for $10,000.

The event raised a staggering $320,000 to assist the British team in winning its 37 medals.

S

SCHARY, DORE
Writer, Director, Producer

During my tenure at MGM Dore Schary was head of production. Born in Newark, New Jersey in 1905, Schary had worked as an actor, journalist, publicist, and playwright before coming to Hollywood in the early 1930s. After establishing himself as a successful screenwriter – sharing an Academy Award for the original story for *Boys Town* (1938) – he became a producer, rising through the studio ranks until he was named chief of production at MGM in 1948.

On what I believe to be a unique occasion, he assembled the entire publicity and advertising departments for a summit meeting in 1955, to outline the studio's policy regarding its program of films. At that time, *Blackboard Jungle* was the hit movie and was selected to be shown at the Cannes Film Festival. Claire Booth Luce, the U.S. Ambassador to France, declared the film to be a fictional account of happenings in American schools and objected to its being presented at the festival. Schary defended the studio's policy of producing films that reflected the genuine American way of life, and held up major newspaper front pages headlining the truth of the movie. We were told to spread the word defending the studio's position.

We did, and the film was greeted very enthusiastically.

SECRET OF SANTA VITTORIA, THE
Feature film (1969)

My sole experience with producer Stanley Kramer was as a unit publicist on this less notable motion picture. It boasted a 100% European cast of Anthony Quinn, Anna Magnani, Virna Lisi, Hardy Kruger, and Eduardo

Ciannelli. It was a World War II comedy based on the Robert Crichton book, involving the townspeople of the titular settlement hiding one million bottles of wine from the occupying Germans.

They worked by night, digging tunnels and erecting brick walls in caves, which originally acted as storage facilities.

It was another interesting departure from the filmmaker who'd brought us *High Noon, The Defiant Ones, The Caine Mutiny, Guess Who's Coming to Dinner*, and *Judgment at Nuremberg*. Happily, Stanley would always reminisce about these films with many apocryphal anecdotes, to the delight of his cast and crew, and this engendered warmth and affection throughout the many weeks of shooting.

From his stories I felt it apparent that he was a "man with a mission" to agitate and disturb racism in *The Defiant Ones*; nuclear war in *On The Beach;* and paraplegics in the Brando film *The Men*. He never seemed to tackle the same theme twice. Though to ensure he wasn't typecast as a "message film" director, he'd then go off and direct something like *It's A Mad, Mad, Mad, Mad, World* to show his diversity.

He spoke of his love for Spencer Tracy in their four films together. *Guess Who's Coming to Dinner* was the most difficult, he explained, because the star was uninsurable. Both Katherine Hepburn and Kramer had to forego their salaries, and after Tracy filmed the final scene – a great speech at the end of the movie – he died 10 days later.

Going back to our film, which was probably more entertaining than socially important, the theme involved wine, and as such, Kramer managed to secure the collaboration of local vintners, and cast and crew were happy at the end of a day's filming to be greeted with bottles of their finest product. This resulted in many sing-a-longs and parties would continue well into the night.

Strange but true, the cast who regularly enjoyed bottles of wine were mostly Italian and never once delayed production, as they said they were used to this level of alcoholic intake – it was in fact part of their daily ritual!

The movie critics were not too favorable, stating it was amusing but far too long at two and a quarter hours.

At 65 Kramer left Hollywood for good, settling in Seattle where he wrote a column for the leading newspaper there. He died in 2001.

SENNES, FRANK
Entertainment impresario

After graduating from high school, Frank Sennes worked as an entertainment manager for several dance halls and resorts in Ohio and Pennsylvania, booking stars such as Guy Lombardo and Rudy Vallee. In 1930 he moved to California where he became the manager of Hollywood Gardens, a nightclub where he gave movie star Betty Grable her first break.

Sennes then moved to Las Vegas in 1949 and became entertainment director of the Desert Inn Hotel when it opened the following year. He later served in a similar capacity at the Stardust, Frontier, and Holiday Casino resorts.

In 1953 he opened the Moulin Rouge in Hollywood, which was, at the time, the biggest nightclub, restaurant, and showroom in America. Frank had approached me twice to handle his nightspot in LA during my tenure at MGM. In late 1955, having gone freelance, I decided to try my hand in a very different type of publicity.

The Moulin Rouge seated 900 patrons and one could attend the lavish show plus have dinner and a cocktail for just $5.50 plus tax. This was an immediate hit and I spent many nights watching Donn Arden's spectacular Paris-style revue, with a parade of showgirls, all staged at the Desert Inn. The revolving stage, the only one in Los Angeles at that time, allowed scenes to be changed in a matter of seconds.

Sennes recognized that the success of his supper club would be dependent on tourism, and therefore assigned me the task of creating an event that would get nationwide attention. I discovered that the Emmy Awards had never been staged as a dinner show on network TV, and after three meetings with the TV Academy and its president Don Defore, I made a deal for the 7th annual event that almost got me chased out of town.

It was agreed that the telecast would take place preceding the regular Moulin Rouge show on March 7 1955. There would be a three-course filet mignon dinner and dancing on stage before and after the telecast utilizing the club's large orchestra – and all this for the unheard of price of $2 per head. How could the TV Academy refuse this?

Sennes went berserk when he realized I had committed him to the low cost and said that it would bankrupt him. It took me many hours to convince him what the coast to coast TV show would have cost, and in one evening he would receive more publicity than any six-month campaign promoting his nightclub. With cameras covering the exterior of the building and three major Moulin Rouge plugs during the commercials, the club would be established nationally.

Thankfully, my instincts proved right, and following the broadcast reservations immediately increased by 60% – I had survived the gamble.

Having over a thousand Academy members and their guests attend when the capacity of the theater was only 900 posed another problem. We had to find tables and chairs to be placed on the top level of the theater. The fire department created a major hurdle at the eleventh hour and the head of the Hollywood branch, a stickler for the law, became extremely irate and threatened to close us down for trying to accommodate an extra 100 people. I tried to reason with him, unsuccessfully, and ended up asking his advice on how I was going to send Lucille Ball, Red Skelton, Danny Thomas, and Milton Berle out onto the street. Nothing would wash with him. I had an idea though. I escorted him to meet Frank Sennes in his

My letter of thanks.

office, situated two stories overhead with a great view of the stage. There, Frank kept him a prisoner for the entire show and the evening continued without interruption!

The papers and magazines were full of coverage: great reviews stating that a dinner awards show was less formal, more intimate, and the ratings were outstanding.

But the fire chief wasn't one to let go a grudge and Sennes was hauled into court. After the judge heard the evidence he had no option but to dismiss the case as nobody had thought to take an actual count of the number of attendees!

This, together with an explanation that the fire captain could view the entire theater from above, witnessing no crowding with the aisles being kept clear, was proof enough that there were no hazards.

SCHNEIDER, ROMY
Actress

My one memorable encounter with the glamorous Austrian actress occurred during a visit to Rome in 1970. I was summoned by director Joseph Losey to his rented villa 75 kilometres outside the capital to discuss a campaign.

He had been filming *The Go-Between* and I arrived on the day he staged a wrap party. Anybody who was anybody in Rome was invited. It was quite a night, consequently, it wasn't until around 1am that Joe began discussing an advertising campaign. As we had rather too much to drink, any thoughts of creative ideas promptly vanished.

Meanwhile, Romy kept telling Joe that she wished to return to her hotel – The Hassler – and he thundered out loud: "Jerry, you are at the Hotel De La Ville next door, call a taxi and take Romy home."

Our ride into Rome took the best part of an hour, and I was looking forward to a nice long chat with the actress en route. The cab arrived, we got in, and she promptly fell asleep in my lap; and that was the end of our first and only meeting. I didn't get to ask her any of the questions racing around my head!

SHAKESPEARE IN LOVE
Feature film (1998)

I'm invited to a lot of screenings in the build-up to the awards season, and try to like every film I see, as I know the sheer hard work that goes into creating them; but when I saw *Shakespeare In Love* I was blown away. I knew Miramax had a big hit on their hands, and a strong Oscar contender.

The actors shone in their roles: Gwyneth Paltrow, Joseph Fiennes, Tom Wilkinson, and a host of British character actors who probably told their agents they'd kill to be in the movie.

Period drama isn't always the easiest seller, and so I knew I had to create awareness for it with as many members of the Academy as possible.

I decided to sit in on some of the screenings that had been organized for the Screen Actors Guild. My gut instinct was that here is a film that actors everywhere would love to be in – wonderful dialogue and luscious settings are things they all look for when evaluating a screenplay.

With my feelings confirmed – they all loved it – I suggested to Miramax that we should gear the advertising towards the actors' branch of the Academy, happily also the largest voting group.

I was absolutely delighted when I heard it received thirteen nominations – just one short of the record held by *All About Eve*. It won seven, including Best Picture and Best Actress for Gwyneth Paltrow – and we all remember that acceptance speech!

SHERMAN, ALLAN
Song parodist

There are times in a publicist's life when one takes on a client with some misgivings, and you kind of know it will all probably end sooner rather than later.

Such was the case of Allan Sherman, who was about to record his first long playing album featuring a song that was the hit of his personal appearance gigs at nightspots around the country. Titled "Hallo Muddah. Hallo Faddah," it spoofed his childhood experiences at summer camp.

His radio and TV appearances certainly charmed Warner Bros. records, and I helped in the media campaigns with an emphasis on the Hollywood trade papers.

For his upcoming six months' anniversary with Warner's – during which he pretty much centred his whole act around that one song – he was booked into the Hollywood Bowl on a Friday night as a solo attraction. To my horror, I discovered that two weeks prior to the concert the sale of tickets was less than 4,000 – for a 17,000 capacity! I spoke with Allan and said we needed to come up with a promotion which was amusing enough to obtain space in the local papers. Warner's weren't going to pay for it, so I told Allan it was definitely worth him taking a punt on spending a few dollars to promote himself. He agreed, so I hired a photographer and ordered half a cake and half a candle, and we did a photo call halfway up the Bowl for his "half anniversary." It was all tongue in cheek and really grabbed the attention of the newspapers who all ran with the story – and tickets sales soared.

When I picked up the bill for the specially designed cake, from Ralphs Grocery section of a main Hollywood supermarket, it was $16. I thought he was joking when Allan said, "Well as we only used half a cake I am only going to pay you back $8."

My intuition had been proved correct, though more was to come.

Allan had been signed to headline in Las Vegas and thought I should attend his debut celebration dinner – at my own expense, naturally. I arrived on a Friday evening and discovered that he had neither reserved (as promised) a room nor a table for the event. I went backstage to see him and, in a very brief conversation, he said that he would see me for breakfast on Sunday morning, as his Saturday had already been booked.

Not being a gambler I reluctantly wasted my time in Vegas, avoiding casinos (which is not easy in that city) until our meeting.

Sunday came around, I arrived at his hotel and Allan greeted me with, "My friends tell me I am not getting the right kind of publicity."

"Do your friends tell you that you have never changed your act, and even now for your Las Vegas debut you have the same material?" I replied.

There was a long pause as Allan thought of something to say, but before he could I did something I have never done before, I said to him:

"I do not have to stand here and be treated so shabbily. You are fired."

SPIELBERG STEVEN
Director, Producer, Writer

My first contact with "the great one" occurred while I was representing a small independent special effects company in Hollywood in the late 1960s. They had an 8-minute short called *Amblin* which they wanted to promote within the trade papers. I met the director, a very young Spielberg, who came to my office and revealed how he'd produced this very creative film. Whatever happened to him?!

We met twice again while I was producing specials for *On the Film Scene* at Z Channel. I still have the footage of his interviews. He was most revealing in discussing *Close Encounters of the Third Kind*.

"I like to make movies for audiences hoping this will open their hearts. I am an optimist and never defend myself against criticism. I was a great fan of the French director Francois Truffaut and cast him in *Encounters* as the wide-eyed master of ceremonies. His first day of shooting was very uncomfortable for him and I suggested that we change places and I read the lines, and eventually the nervousness disappeared."

They had many long discussions on the types of movies one should make, and Truffaut suggested that Spielberg should make a film about kids, and as a result *E.T.* became a reality.

"I thought *E.T.* would be a sweet, small movie and was surprised at its huge success" Spielberg confessed. "I felt that with fantasy one must have had to have established great reality for acceptance."

SMITH, JACLYN
Actress

Jaclyn was regarded as one of Hollywood's true beauties, and I commenced my association with her in 1978. For over 20 years we had a great relationship, from *Charlie's Angels* through many mini-series and movies for TV.

First and foremost came her two children, Gaston and Spencer Margaret. Any decisions regarding the many scripts submitted depended on the answer to her first question, "Where does the filming take place?" She refused to be separated from the two kids, and rarely, if ever, accepted anything where she could not be home at night or have them with her on location.

Jaclyn Smith in *Charlie's Angels* mode (with Farrah Fawcett and Kate Jackson).

This may have been the reason why she never really attained the rarefied heights of stardom, although she was regarded as "The Queen of Mini-Series" by the nation's TV critics. Her priorities showed a rare attitude in Hollywood where so many tragedies had occurred in family lives. Her ratings were generally high whether she played an ambassador, lawyer, doctor, or killer, and her presence on screen was captivating. The diversity of roles was never ending and many were in sharp contrast to her Kelly Garrett role in *Charlie's Angels*.

Apart from her acting career, Jaclyn created a video for self improvement with the emphasis on a healthy lifestyle, targeting today's busy woman. This was coupled with her signature line of women's clothing and accessories for the Kmart national chain of stores. They certainly made her a lady of diversified interests and talents.

Even though publicists are not allowed to solicit employment for actors, it is common practice to network within the industry, suggesting roles in future projects for one's clients. For example, I represented the writer Sidney Sheldon, who was preparing his *Rage of Angels* project for NBC, and I felt that his uncertainty about his lead actress casting could be solved by his meeting Jaclyn.

As I was also representing the noted British automobile company, Rolls Royce, it occurred to me that I could accomplish a triple play by combing three elements here.

Sidney, who always maintained houses in the multi-million-dollar range, had just purchased a fabulous mansion with an extremely large and architecturally superb forecourt. It could easily accommodate 20 cars.

With Sidney Sheldon.

I arranged to "borrow" the forecourt from Sidney for a cocktail party for press and celebrities to be introduced to the new Rolls Royce models.

This was the perfect opportunity to introduce Jaclyn to Sidney – and she was subsequently cast. They got on so well that she was then rehired by Sidney for his next venture, *Windmill of the Gods*.

It is always a sad occasion when one parts company with a client, and our relationship came to an end for the sole reason Jaclyn hired a new manager who insisted on a change. It of course saddened me, but we parted on good terms, and I have always had the philosophy that if a client can find somebody who can give him or her a love, dedication, and enthusiasm greater than mine, I would assist them in moving.

STACK, ROBERT
Actor

Robert Stack was the good-looking kid who kissed Deanna Durbin on screen for the first time in the movie *First Love,* and gained notoriety throughout the world.

Well, it was 1939 after all!

It is difficult to believe that Universal Studios declined the offer from *Life* magazine to publish this romantic interlude photograph on the cover; the executives at the studio were concerned that the public would regard the embrace as scandalous and might possibly boycott the new film. How times have changed.

Having seen the movie in London as a child, I could never have imagined that twenty years later I would be representing the star. It just goes to show that you should reach for your dreams, as they can come true.

We met under very strange, but fortuitous circumstances. As the entertainment editor of the *Beverly Hills Citizen* I had just been to interview MGM singing star Jeanette McDonald, and following the meeting walked out on to South Beverly Drive in Beverly Hills and there noticed a brand new red Jaguar XK 120 parked. At the same moment a meter maid was approaching – I saw the meter read "expired."

I felt pity for the unfortunate soul whose new beauty seemed destined for a traffic violation fine. After inserting a dime, a dashing hunk of a movie star rushed out noticing my good deed for the day. Robert Stack's first words were

"I rushed in to get change and there you are saving me a citation and a fine. Thanks a lot."

We struck up a conversation lasting 15 minutes, talking about the business and so forth, and Bob invited me up to his Bel Air mansion – for a full-scale interview in my paper as a reward.

There, we talked and talked and talked. Bob told me he was fifth-generation Californian and had grown up among the many motion picture, concert, opera, and radio favorites who lived in the area. Most of the biggest names were guests of the family during his childhood years, so it was only natural that his first and only ambition was to follow in the footsteps of these people.

Bob's mother, known to her friends as Betsy, was an icon of Los Angeles society, and when she divorced his father, James Langford Stack, she took the one-year-old offspring to Europe where his first language became French.

I discovered so many things about the family, such as in 1912 Betsy was on her first trip to Europe with her father and they had booked return passage on the SS Titanic. She begged her father to stay on a little longer in Paris, to do some more shopping, and saved their lives.

His father eventually became a noted advertising executive and created the famous slogan "The Beer That Made Milwaukee Famous."

The Mortal Storm (1940) and *To Be or Not to Be* (1942) were two notable features in Bob's early career, and both were somewhat anti-German. So, when the Nazis uncovered the hiding place of Anne Frank they discovered a fan mail photograph of Stack, who was immediately placed on the their "death watch" list. Quite a worrying thought.

Bob's movie career was halted during the war while he received a commission in the U.S. Navy, where he became an "aerial gunnery instructor." The Stack family's military history included a cousin who bore the rank of rear admiral, an uncle who became a commander, and seven other relatives all on sea duty.

His movie work resumed in 1947 and included his working with such luminaries as Elizabeth Taylor, Jane Powell, Bing Crosby, and John Wayne.

That was one of Bob's most interesting stories; Wayne wasn't acting, but producing, and the movie was *The Bullfighter and the Lady*, directed by his friend Budd Boetticher – who incidentally was a former matador. Though Bob had no experience in bullfighting, his friend (director) Andrew McLaglen invited him to Mexico under the premise of a junket – Bob never realized that it was a pretext to audition him. Observing his reactions to entering a bullring and in particular, noting whether he flinched under pressure, director Boetticher was extremely impressed with Bob and immediately offered him the lead. He headed for Mexico City and signed up for a month's lessons from some of the top toreadors.

The film came about after Herbert Yates, the head of Republic Pictures, who had made many successful westerns with John Wayne, in a moment of weakness, succumbed to Wayne's wish to produce a feature on bullfighting. Not wanting to alienate his box office star, the project was (reluctantly) set up with Wayne as producer. Yates hoped that a mediocre publicity and advertising campaign would mean the film would fair modestly, at best, so that Wayne would not be tempted to give up acting in favor of a producing career. Ironically, the film has become a classic and is shown in festivals around the world.

Wayne, who was as tough off screen as on, never forgave Yates for attempting to sabotage the movie's chances, and never again associated with him or his studio.

My first job on Robert Stack's behalf took place in 1955 when he played Kyle Hadley in Universal's *Written on the Wind*, co-starring Lauren Bacall and Rock Hudson. In those days the studios arranged sneak previews for films that showed promised, and these were run without viewers ever knowing beforehand what the title was or

Me with Bob Stack.

who the principal stars were. One such screening for *Wind* was held at the Encino, a small California theater, on a Friday night. Bob and his wife Rosemarie invited his costars Hudson, Bacall, and Dorothy Malone to the house for cocktails prior to the screening, then we all drove to the theater for the audience's reaction to the drama.

The theaete crowd mobbed the actors at the end of the film and it took us 40 minutes to leave the lobby.

That was a good omen.

Dorothy Malone and Bob were both nominated. Dorothy won the Oscar for Best Supporting Actress while Bob, sadly, missed out to Anthony Quinn in *Viva Zapata* – even though the *Variety* poll voted him the top award.

An invitation by Bob's mother, Betsy, to her palatial mansion was a privilege regarded akin to visit royalty. I was one of the privileged and she embraced us all with the warmest smile I have ever seen. Bob's den there consisted of the trophies he'd won in skeet shooting and for the speed records he broke in hydroplaning. He had in fact broken many world records by the tender age of 15, and his collection of guns was the envy of most sports enthusiasts. In 1971 he was inducted into the National Skeet

The Untouchable Robert Stack, in his most famous role.

Shooting Hall of Fame, and in 1976 helped raise funds for the U.S. team to go to Montreal for the summer Olympic games, where he appeared as a guest participant in the national qualifying competition.

Parties at Betsy's house were always colorful. Movie stars were everywhere! Bob was the perfect host and I was fascinated to be able talk informally and friendly to those I had adored from afar.

Bob's movie career was beginning to rocket, but with the advent of TV, and one show in particular, his rise to superstardom was accelerated even more.

In the late 1950s Desi Arnaz, thanks to the success of I *Love Lucy*, with his wife Lucille Ball, bought and operated a studio called DESILU. They decided to produce a new one hour tv drama series entitled *The Untouchables,* based on the life of Eliot Ness. Bob was delighted to be cast in the role, and while he hoped it would be a success, he could not have possibly anticipated just how big it would become.

From 1959-63 he became a household name and won an Emmy Award in the process. Of course, Bob's star was high and it lead to a great many wonderful offers both in features and TV. I worked with him throughout, representing him as a client, and we had great fun all the way. He was a very genuine guy and always played it straight.

He became a household name (and face) all over again in the 1980s, as from the late part of the decade through the massively popular *Unsolved Mysteries* TV series.

It was with a heavy heart that I learned of Bob's death while at the Cannes Film Festival in May 2003. His beautiful wife Rosemarie called to give me the tragic news – he'd suffered a heart attack. I realized that my life would never be the same without his smile, warmth, and regular chats over the telephone. It hasn't been.

SUNDAY BLOODY SUNDAY
Feature film (1971)

[see also **JACKSON, GLENDA**]

At certain times in life, one gets a nice surprise. Mine came with a call from United Artists concerning this movie in which Glenda Jackson was starring.

They had never considered the film as awards potential, but the New York opening certainly made them realize otherwise. They decided to open in LA within a week, and wanted me to prepare a campaign.

Previews were set up in LA, and to be honest, we got more of a mixed reaction to the story line where Peter Finch plays a Jewish gay psychiatrist who loves Murray Head, a bisexual artist who in turn loves both Finch and heterosexual Jackson.

With Glenda Jackson on the PR trail in Los Angeles.

One journalist, who attended one of the previews, asked why director John Schlesinger chose to make Finch Jewish – as though it mattered in the grand scheme of things. The director replied: "I am a Jewish homosexual, and some of my friends are psychiatrists of the same persuasion. Would you prefer it if I made him a Catholic?"

There was no reply.

For three days, I escorted John to every TV chat show, radio station, and many of the previews. So exhausted he was, that he booked himself into a rest home and said "Jerry, directing a movie is a breeze compared to having to publicize it."

John told me that Peter Finch had trouble with what was to be the first scene in the movie, with a woman patient (June Brown), saying he felt the character was introduced as "very cold and uncaring" and that wasn't the way to open the movie.

Finch felt his character should be provided with a scene showing him in a better, more commanding situation. Therefore, Penelope Gilliatt wrote a page which now opens the film, where he is examining an older gentleman (Richard Pearson) who is worried about a pain. The phone keeps ringing during the exam and Hirsh (Finch) has to deal with it. In fact, Finch handles this scene so well – the embarrassment of having to beg for your lover to call back in a minute or two and all that this implies. Compassion and sincerity was written all over Finch's face as he tells the patient that he doesn't have cancer.

John received Oscar nominations for direction and Penelope Gilliatt for her screenplay. The two main leads Glenda and Finchie were Oscar nominated for their performances too.

TOWN WITHOUT PITY
Feature film (1961)

This film was financed on the star, Kirk Douglas' name. He plays a lawyer (Steve Garrett) defending four American GI's stationed in Germany, who are all accused of raping a local girl (played by Christine Kaufmann).

The U.S. Army, the villagers, and even the girl's family are more interested in revenge than in the welfare of the distraught victim. Garrett is faced with the dilemma of destroying the girl on the witness stand in order to save the lives of his clients.

The trial is the dramatic centre of the movie, though director Gottfried Reinhardt's direction did little to create the dramatic intensity that the script and story suggested. A potentially powerful drama limped along and misfired.

The most exciting time came when Douglas disappeared for three days. Everyone wondered what was happening, until we heard that he'd been in Paris for the premiere of *Spartacus*. It's a pity he never invited me!

TURNER, KATHLEEN
Actress

Though I had nothing to do with the production, my brother-in-law, Bill Kenney, was production designer on *Body Heat*, and that is where I met Kathleen Turner. It was her first film and I thought that an interview on the cable station, Z Channel, which I was heavily involved with, would help introduce her to the Hollywood scene. She readily agreed.

I must admit she struck me as looking somewhat like a young Lauren Bacall. In fact, I later learned that upon meeting the legendary Miss Bacall, she introduced herself by saying, "Hi, I'm the young you."

I was fascinated to learn that by the tender age of 14 Kathleen had already resided in five different countries, as her father, Richard, was a foreign service diplomat, who had actually been imprisoned by the Japanese during WWII.

While in high school in London she excelled as a gymnast but chose to enrol at the Central School Of Speech and Drama in the city. It proved a good grounding, as she told me.

"After returning to New York I was fortunate to work on *The Doctors*, a popular soap opera. It was great training as we filmed five shows a week and I featured in at least a third of each show. It gave me an instant recognition, though the scripts could be best described as mediocre, and after about seven months I decided I should move on to something a bit more challenging. Luckily, I was cast in a Broadway show called *Gemini*."

Body Heat launched her film career, and other exciting roles soon followed in *Romancing The Stone, Prizzi's Honor, Undercover Blues*, and she also provided the voice(uncredited) of sexy Jessica Rabbit in *Who Framed Roger Rabbit* (1988).

Later Kathleen was considered for the lead in *Basic Instinct* (1992), but it went to Sharon Stone.

She received a lifetime achievement award from the Savannah College of Art and Design at the Savannah Film Festival in October 2004, and was nominated for Broadway's 1990 Tony Award as Best Actress (Play) for portraying Maggie the Cat in a revival of Tennessee Williams' *Cat on a Hot Tin Roof*. We'll be hearing a lot more from Miss Turner.

U

ULLMANN, LIV
Actress

I met Liv in 1971 at the Oscars – well, there's a bit more to it. She was represented by agent Paul Kohner, and I had worked with a number of his clients over the years, so we knew each other pretty well.

Early one morning, just after the nominations had been announced for the 43rd Academy Awards, Paul called me.

"Jerry, I need a great favor. You're the one man who can help."

I listened intently.

"My client Ingmar Bergman will be receiving the Irving G. Thalberg Award for a lifetime of achievement in filmmaking. Ingmar does not fly, so I have arranged for Liv Ullmann to accept the award on his behalf."

"Okay." I said.

There was a brief pause before Paul continued. "Would you escort her to the ceremony?" I thought I'd misheard him, but no, he was adamant in his request.

"But why me?" I asked, "Given all the possible Hollywood stars you could ask?"

He explained that Liv was the great director's companion and it would be inappropriate for her to be seen on the arm of a big star, but he knew I'd look after her, and her "publicist" accompanying her wouldn't cause tongues to wag.

April 15 is a day most American's hate, as it is tax-due day with the IRS, but for me it was a day I was so looking forward to – the Academy Awards.

I dutifully escorted the Norwegian star from the Beverly Hills Hotel to the Dorothy Chandler Pavilion in downtown LA. We had a good 45 minutes to chat in the limousine and, fortunately, as I am an aficionado of foreign films – and knew of *Personna* and *Cries and Whispers* – we got on really well.

With Liv Ullman.

Following the ceremony we went to the Governor's Ball, and I have never been photographed as much in my life!

It was two years after this that I met the Norwegian Angel again (as she was dubbed),and again it was at the Oscars, where my client Roger Moore and she were asked to present the Best Actor award. When Marlon Brando's name was read out, a young Native American girl named Sacheen Little Feather announced that he was rejecting the Oscar due to the way Native Americans were being treated by Hollywood.

It was a rather embarrassing episode, and as no one else took the award it was left to Roger to look after it. He took it home for safe keeping, and while awaiting someone from the Academy to collect it, his daughter Deborah suggested that he keep it. Roger explained that he couldn't, to which she replied "Well let's give it to Michael Caine then!"

Some 15 years later I was attending the annual Montreal film festival. I stepped into an elevator at the Four Seasons Hotel, and there was Liv! With instant recognition she hugged me tightly, much to the bemusement of the others in there. They must have wondered who the hell I was! Liv was there promoting a film, not as a star, but as a director.

UNFORGIVEN
Feature film (1992)

This marked a return to the western genre for Clint Eastwood and Hollywood. Many believed the Western had had its day. In the USA alone, the film grossed over $80 million dollars – the genre was certainly anything but dead!

The film was backed by Warner Bros., who weren't quite sure of its chances at the Academy Awards. They didn't believe it would make any money, let alone win an award! After much internal discussion, it was felt they had to at least try, and I was drafted in to assist with the campaign.

On the night it won four Oscars: Best Picture, Best Director (Eastwood), Best Supporting Actor (Gene Hackman) and Best Editing (Joel Cox).

Of course, everyone was quick to claim credit for the film – a successful baby has many mothers. Yet little did they know the back story that twenty years or so earlier, David Webb Peoples wrote the original script, then called *The William Munny Killings*. He sent it to Gene Hackman, who turned it down. A short time after, Clint read the script and bought the rights, he then waited until he felt old enough to do the part justice.

Clint next approached Gene Hackman about a supporting role and again Hackman, convinced he'd already done too many violent films, turned down the offer. But Clint persuaded him that the film would actually make a powerful anti-violence statement.

Richard Harris was next to be cast. Curiously, he was watching *High Plains Drifter* on TV when Clint phoned him to offer the part of English Bob.

A stickler for authenticity, Clint wouldn't allow modern vehicles on the set, which – like *High Plains Drifter* – comprised both interiors and exteriors.

Something else you might not know about Clint is that he is a very talented musician. Although the score was arranged by Lennie Niehaus, the main theme was written by Clint himself.

[see also **EASTWOOD, CLINT**]

V

VALENTI, JACK
Head of MPAA

I never anticipated that Jack would ever retire as head of the Motion Picture Association of America, but in 2004 at the age of 82, he decided to hang up his hat.

Texas born and Harvard educated, Jack was a wartime bomber pilot, advertising agency founder, and political consultant before he radically changed the landscape of the American film and television industry.

In 1955, while heading up the advertising/political consulting agency of Weekley & Valenti, he met the then Majority Leader of the U.S. Senate, Lyndon B. Johnson. Valenti's agency was in charge of the press during the visit of President Kennedy and Vice President Johnson to Texas. Valenti was in the motorcade in Dallas on November 22, 1963. Within hours of the assassination of John F. Kennedy, Valenti was on Air Force One flying back to Washington, as the first newly hired special assistant to the new president.

On June 1, 1966, Valenti resigned his White House post to become only the third man in MPAA history to become its leader.

In 1968 he created the ratings system which he hoped would supersede all the various censorship boards around the country, and make one universal method by which films could be judged by the letters G, PG, R, and X. These were later modified to G, PG, PG 13, R, and NC 17.

Jack attended the Cannes Film Festival every year, and we used to have rooms near each other at the Majestic Hotel. He was the most approachable executive I have ever known. On one occasion we had a drink in the bar and he told me of his love for movies. "Jerry, movies are what most people want, no matter what the delivery system is – cable, VCR, DVD, free or pay-tv. Theater-going is the best of all however, and I feel people will always go to the movies above any other choice, to enjoy the social experience and enjoy watching a film with an audience."

Jack encountered a backlash from Academy members in 2003 when, in a bid to counter piracy, the MPAA decided to recommend to its members that they did not send out "screeners" (the DVDs of those motion pictures which distributors deem potential Oscar nominees), which were the biggest source of piracy. Many criticized Jack for making a hasty decision that would have serious knock-on effects when it came to voting for the all-important Oscars.

Jack sat down to talk with the industry representatives and came up with the solution of encoding "screeners" in future years, and only Academy members would have a DVD player compatible with those discs from 2005 onwards. Hopefully it will see a mass reduction in piracy, without impinging on Oscar voting.

VANISHING, THE
Feature film (1988)

Not to be confused with the 1993 remake, this Dutch film resulted in the Academy changing its rules! The kidnapping suspense drama directed by George Sluizer was initially accepted in the Foreign Language category, as submitted by the Netherlands. One of the rules therein stated that 50% of the dialogue had to be the language of the country of submission. A lot of the film was shot in France, and consequently the director decided he could not expect his audience to accept French peasants speaking Dutch. He had them speak French, and used Dutch subtitles.

The film was eliminated from competition as a result.

The following year however, a rule change was made where the proviso was made that if a film's storyline specified settings in another country, and therefore another language was incorporated, then this would be permitted. Alas I had failed in my attempt to mount an Oscar campaign. However, box office returns were good enough to warrant a Hollywood remake with Jeff Bridges, though that version flopped!

VAUGHN, ROBERT
Actor

I first met Robert at the Players' Ring Theater in Los Angeles when he was appearing in the Calder Willingham play *End as a Man* (1957). He gave such a great performance that I suggested the theater's press agent invite producer Sam Spiegel to see the show. My reasoning was that if he was excited about Vaughn's performance, he would consider him for the lead in the film version, which he was setting up.

The famed filmmaker did indeed attend, and said he would consider Vaughn. I read in the *Hollywood Reporter* the following day that Ben Gazzara had been signed for the film, retitled *The Strange One,* as he had created the part on Broadway! However, my efforts were soon rewarded when Robert hired me; he was set to star with Paul Newman and Barbara Rush in *The Young Philadelphians* at Warner Bros.

This was to be the start of a 22-year association and we certainly started with a bang. I felt his reviews for the movie could possibly see him in contention for an Oscar nomination, so I planned a campaign. To my astonishment most of the press had never seen the film.

Lo and behold, the Academy nominations were announced and Robert Vaughn was a nominee in the Best Supporting Actor category alongside Hugh Griffith, Arthur O'Connell, George C. Scott, and Ed Wynn. This was a marvellous beginning to our friendship.

Films such as *The Magnificent Seven*, *The Towering Inferno*, and *Julius Caesar* were a joy for me to publicize, and when he starred as *The Man From U.N.C.L.E.*, I was excited that his career as a movie and TV star had come full circle.

Most people were unaware that he was the first actor to oppose the war in Vietnam, and both MGM and NBC were scared to death that this would force the cancellation of the series – especially as he went around the country making inflammatory speeches at college campuses.

With Robert Vaughn and Senator Wayne Morse.

The syndicated columnists Novak and Evans crucified him, stating that he was un-American. This led to an accidental meeting with President Lyndon Johnson at a Democratic fundraiser in New York, who remarked "So you are the troublemaker."

However, Robert survived all the harangues and in no time the mood of the country changed and he was applauded for his stand which was so unpopular at the outset.

Robert was very dedicated to the Democratic Party and his idol was Jack Kennedy. Whenever possible he would travel the country making speeches in favor of the future president, and subsequently about the Vietnam War.

W

WILDER, BILLY
Writer, Director, Producer

I had known Billy Wilder for over 40 years. As a journalist I covered his productions of *Witness for the Prosecution* through *Some Like it Hot*, *The Apartment*, and *Irma La Douce*. His sets were always very friendly and happy-go-lucky.

Born on June 22, 1906, he often said he was proud to have the same natal day as John Dillinger, who was the notorious gangster of the 1930s. At one time he considered a feature on the hoodlum and I

With the great Billy Wilder.

feel that he substituted the St. Valentine's Day massacre of *Some Like it Hot* instead.

His acerbic humor was always refreshing, as he poked fun at the industry, his films, and indeed, himself. He was irreverent to an extreme and no subject was considered exempt from his brilliant vocabulary. His partner on so many hits was a chain-smoking character, I.A.L Diamond, whom everyone called Izzy. They would plot their off-beat ideas in an old-fashioned office in the heart of Beverly Hills, known as the Writers and Artists Building. Then during their great days with the Mirisch-United Artists partnership they also had offices on the old Samuel Goldwyn lot (now Warner's Hollywood), where they shot many of their great hits.

Billy was very philosophical about many of his movies, even when they were not successful. In 1981 he made *Buddy, Buddy* with his two favorite actors, Jack Lemmon and Walter Matthau. The film was a failure everywhere, with the exception of Italy, where it was a huge success. Billy knew that it was not really up to his usual high standards, but couldn't understand how it could have possibly achieved such grosses in the small European country. Upon discovering why – namely the dubbing of his film into Italian, he realized it obviously improved in translation!

After I had seen the remake of one of his greatest triumphs, *Sabrina*, I encountered Billy at a Hollywood party and discussed my negative feelings. He made the following comment:

"When I made *Sabrina* I used two male stars of equal status, Humphrey Bogart and William Holden, and the moviegoer could not guess who was going to get the girl. In this new version, Harrison Ford received $15 million dollars for his performance and Gregg Kinnear got $750,000. Who do you think got the girl?"

Needless to say, the remake was not as successful as the original.

Walter Matthau related a couple of lovely Wilder one liners to me. On having watched a Wilder movie once on TV, Walter said to the director that it was quite probably the worst he'd ever seen. Wilder replied "I made that film over 20 years ago, and just like that girl you went out with then, 20 years later she doesn't look so hot."

Another wonderful Wilder retort occurred after he visited a brothel. He began walking out of the house when a call girl called after him, "What about the money?" He replied "I am an officer in the Austrian Army Reserve and we never accept payment for our services."

Billy, who often described Hollywood as a place that was going into intensive care, enjoyed discussing how the system worked (or didn't). He lamented that lawyers, agents, supermarket operators, and soft drink distributors were the ones who decide what film gets made or not. Scientific computer projections and audience profiles add to the mix and they all come up with the same answer – get Richard Pryor, he's really hot this week.

"The truth is that pictures are part of a gut feeling – that requires you to have guts" he said.

Here are some short takes from a TV special I made with Billy in 1986 on his 80th birthday for Z Channel's *On the Film Scene* show.

On *Some Like It Hot*:

"The idea came to me when I read 'Fanfares of Love', a European book which, after purchasing, I discarded and just utilized the idea of two musicians dressing up as girls for a female dance band. Placing this in the context of the 1920s I was able to juxtapose violence with comedy."

"I considered Sinatra for the Curtis role, but with the signing of Lemmon felt that the chemistry might be too combative."

"I attended a dedication ceremony at the Los Angeles Coliseum for the movement of the Dodgers baseball team from Brooklyn to the West Coast, and was astonished by a speech given by old-time actor Joe E. Brown welcoming the team. I felt that he would be perfect for the movie because of his warm personality. My hunch paid off."

On *Sunset Boulevard*:

"Casting of the lead was critical and we tested old-time star Pola Negri, then an interview was set for Mary Pickford. When I arrived at Picfair, her fabulous home, I had to unpitch my original desire to use her, as I recognized that as 'America's Sweetheart' she would have been miscast as Norma Desmond. Now when one thinks of typecasting, what could have been more perfect than Gloria Swanson who was almost portraying herself? She contacted me for the role and my problem was solved."

Another casting coup took place when Billy later landed Erich Von Stroheim as the butler to Swanson, thus reteaming them, in the lavish extravaganza *Queen Kelly*, which he directed.

On *The Apartment*:

"The idea for the film really came to me years before when I saw David Lean's *Brief Encounter*, which depicted a country doctor (Trevor Howard) having a weekly liaison with a married housewife (Celia Johnson} at his friend's house.

"Fred MacMurray was NOT my first choice, as we had already signed Paul Douglas for the role of the insurance company executive. Three days prior to shooting Douglas suffered a fatal heart attack and I remembered what a great performance MacMurray gave in *Double Indemnity*. It took some time to convince him to take the role, as he had been so identified with family comedies at Disney, and in particular *My Three Sons*. Eventually, thank goodness, he signed."

He continued:

"When I planned to preview the movie for the first time, it occurred to me that I was exposing the film to over a thousand idiots and they would then become experts, telling me whether I had a good or bad movie.

"The executives and producers spend 18 hours a day trying to get the best financial deals for themselves, though they don't spend *that* amount of time and effort making the best picture. Then actors argue about who gets first and second billing, whether the name goes above or below the title…that has more importance than the roles themselves. I feel I am living in the last days of Pompeii."

On *Irma La Douce:*

"There was much concern from the Catholic Church regarding the film's theme, and a priest from the local diocese was assigned for three days to advise and assist us. The first day he was very serious and criticized the décolletage, advising to lengthen the skirts and soften some of the language. The second day he read the two Hollywood trade papers, and on the third day enquired if there were any other movies to which he could be assigned."

When Billy was honored at the American Film Institute (AFI) with their Lifetime Achievement Award, at the dinner both Jessica Lang and Whoopi Goldberg praised him from the stage and expressed how they would like to star as leads in an upcoming movie. Billy responded by saying that he was writing *The Sisters Karamazov* just for them – many forget that Billy was a successful writer too. During his career with co-writer Charles Brackett at Paramount, he always queried the studio about being allowed to direct his own material, but he was continually denied that chance. Finally, the studio bosses relented, fearing they would lose their highly successful writing team. To pacify him, the studio offered him a small film, *The Major and the Minor*, in the hopes that he would give up this notion of trying to compete with the established directors of the day. They expected a flop, and instead the film grossed very well and Ginger Rogers, in a non-dancing role, showed what a splendid actress she had become.

Wilder had a few strange observations regarding Tennessee Williams' play *Suddenly Last Summer*, which Gore Vidal adapted for the screen to star Katharine Hepburn and Elizabeth Taylor.

"Most of us hate making films which insult vast segments of the movie-going public like Jews, Catholics, homosexuals, and the PTA. Here they have defiled one of the vastest segments – the vegetarians." He was, of course, referring to the film's inclusion of cannibalism.

With his death, Hollywood seemed at a loss. Billy had gone. Fortunately, he left us a great legacy – his movies. From the dramatic *Double Indemnity* to the farcical *Some Like it Hot*, all are preserved forever and they will bear testament to his greatness.

WILLIAMS, ESTHER
Actress

As a teenager I would drool over the luscious, sexy actress revelling in her aquatic sequences in MGM extravaganzas. Had I thought, one day, that I would own a swimming pool let alone have Esther Williams christen it, I'd have laughed at myself.

I met Esther by virtue of representing Fernando Lamas, whom I had previously publicized during my days at MGM. One Saturday night

My first meeting with Esther Williams, thanks to our mutual friend Fernanado Lamas (centre).

I was invited to a dinner party at Fernando's house and was unaware that he had started dating his *Dangerous When Wet* costar.

The thrill of sitting across the dining table listening to Esther's stories of happenings on such movies as *Bathing Beauty*, *Ziegfeld Follies*, and *Take Me Out to the Ball Game* with Frank Sinatra and Gene Kelly made me feel like a confidant who was entrusted with secrets never before revealed. I wasn't of course, but that's how special she made you feel.

My pool party with a difference, thanks to Esther Williams.

Several weeks later I invited Fernando to attend the christening of my first ever swimming pool. Little did I realize that he would bring Esther to dedicate the occasion by taking the first dive. Too bad I couldn't afford a movie camera to record this historic event.

Dreams do come true!

WINDSOR, MARIE
Actress

As one of my early publicity clients, I always had a great admiration for Marie. She was a far more talented actress than the casting directors gave her credit for, and was offered roles that barely stretched her at all.

One of the problems in Hollywood was that if you appeared in too many "B" pictures (these no longer exist as their place was usurped by early TV productions) it was extremely difficult to get back into major movies. Such films as *A Narrow Margin* showed her unique versatility, and in an early Stanley Kubrick feature *The Killing* she won a *Look* magazine award.

An interesting situation occurred one day outside the office of a noted "B" movie producer, Robert Lippert. By chance, another Marie, by name Blanchard, arrived and discovered that there had been a mix-up in times for interviews. Both actresses had been promised a role and both given the same meeting time with the producer.

They were so annoyed at being treated so underhandedly that they threatened to go to the Screen Actors Guild.

Lippert was a very shrewd producer and, not wanting SAG on his back, decided to give them both the lead – in a new script. He decided to reverse all the male roles to females, and thus came western *Outlaw Women*, made at a cost of $130,000, and it went on to be one of his biggest successes grossing over one and a half million dollars which, in the mid 1950's, was pretty damn good.

X

XMAS

Is this the happiest time of year? Well, I guess it depends on what one is doing at the time.

For publicists it is a time to start mapping out the Oscar campaigns – and so there isn't a holiday!

When the awards ceremony was brought forward some years ago, a month earlier to February, the voting schedules were brought forward too. In this time to the build up, one has to analyze the competition and avoid direct conflicts with trade advertisements and final screening schedules. One learns to book screening rooms well in advance when you have a possible contender, otherwise you get edged out by others that gain a little voter momentum.

The mailings of DVDs, which compromise the bulk of seductive awareness to the voting members, also had to be moved forward to try and avoid the holidays, hopefully thereby ensuring members who didn't see the films in theatres didn't miss out on receiving this substitute.

For those in town, the major film distributors use the holiday period to showcase their prime candidates in the most popular theatres, complimented by scores of full-page advertisements in the trade papers – "For Academy Consideration."

However, no matter how much campaigning there is, if the voting member has not seen the film, chances of success are slim – and that's what I always preach to companies!

Z

Z CHANNEL

I've made mention, several times, about cable TV's Z Channel. I actually created a series, *On The Film Scene*, for them – what a gig for a movie lover! Introduced in 1974 on the now defunct Theta Cable (owned by Hughes Aircraft and Teleprompter), Z's audience comprised residents of Beverly Hills and the complete west side of Los Angeles, extending into the San Fernando Valley – a big Hollywood catchment.

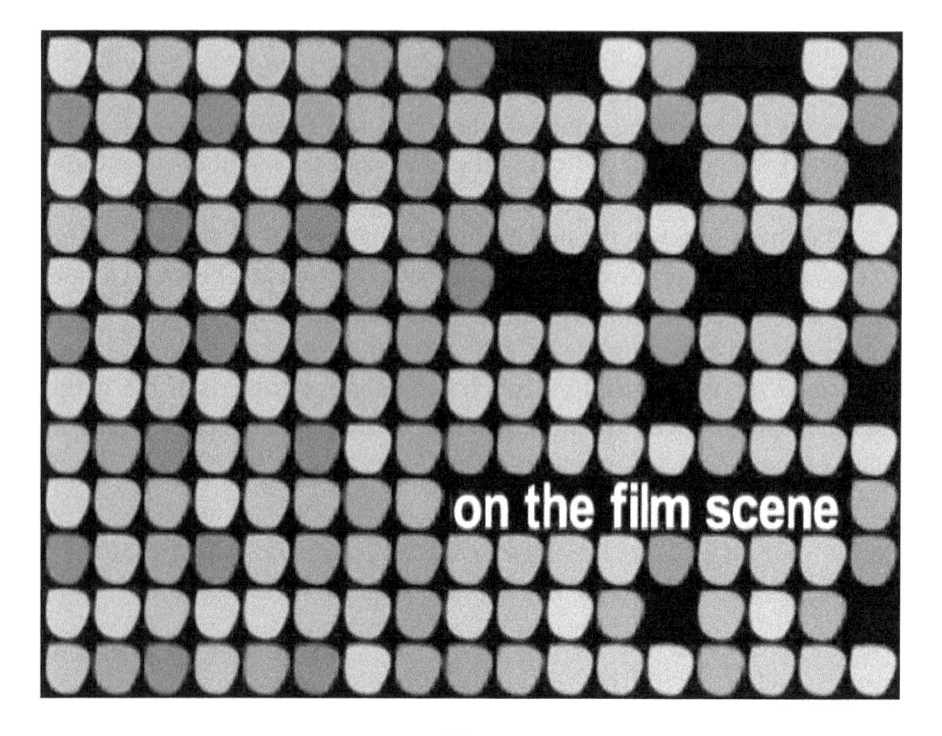

The innovative cable channel became an important marketing tool for motion pictures during the mid 70's to mid 80's. Theta cable became the first pay-TV system in the USA, and one has to remember this was before the introduction of HBO, Showtime, and The Movie Channel. They later, of course, assumed a greater control in movies – which they would produce, co-produce, or part finance – and hence controlled the day and date release of the films on TV, and indeed on which channel they would air!

Theta Cable went from a base of 60,000 subscribers to over 100,000 when Z entered the fray, and everyone rejoiced when other systems in Southern California carried Z programming too. The demographics of Hollywood subscribers working in the entertainment field certainly accounted for its popularity.

To capitalize on our impact on the Hollywood viewership, I approached Z with the idea of doing a "publicity" show and submitted the *On the Film Scene* idea to management. The company's marketing manager, Robert Strock, seized upon it and assisted me in developing the show for the channel.

The main idea was to feature actors or production people who were keen to promote new films, just prior to their release in movie theaters. The studios were mostly cooperative and a who's who of Hollywood from Steven Spielberg and Robert Wise to James Stewart and Warren Beatty were willing guests of the channel.

I signed Charles Champlin, the then arts editor and chief film reviewer for the *Los Angeles Times*, to act as moderator in the many interviews that took place in the studio.

Conversations with noted directors David Lean and Billy Wilder, to name but two, as well as specials around potential Oscar nominees became a highly anticipated annual event on the channel

Our first show commenced with Francis Ford Coppola's *The Conversation*. It was a motion picture that had received overwhelmingly positive reviews, yet was overlooked by the public…and I feared, would be too by Academy members.

As I was representing Gene Hackman, the film's star, at that time, and realizing that 80% of Academy members were in the Z Channel area, I convinced Paramount to let us telecast the film. The film garnered four nominations that year, including Best Screenplay, Best Film and Sound.

Three years later in 1977 we were in the midst of blockbusters such as *Close Encounters of the Third Kind* and *Star Wars*. A friend of mine, Lloyd Leipzig, who represented United Artists, asked us to screen *Annie Hall* on the channel for much the same reasoning I had with *The Conversation*. The film not only won the Oscar for Best Film, but Diane Keaton received the Best Actress Oscar and Woody Allen two Oscars for writing and directing. In a survey, we discovered only 25% of members had seen the film prior to our telecast.

In 1985 I received a nomination for the Cable Ace award for *On the Film Scene*. As the official announcement stated, "To be nominated from a total of 748 entries for the cable industry's highest award is an honor in itself." A year later I decided to produce a special for the channel, compiling some of the most outstanding clips taken from eight years of shows, and here is a summary of that program:

> We see Steven Spielberg, over a span of 7 years, maturing and discussing his approach to filmmaking, and even crediting the great French director Francois Truffaut for the idea of making *ET;*
>
> David Lean discussed the problems of directing epics;
>
> Billy Wilder discussed making flops;
>
> Francis Ford Coppola on his movie *The Conversation;*
>
> John Huston, about how he originally cast Clark Gable and Humphrey Bogart in *The Man Who Would be King,* but couldn't get the financing;
>
> George Burns on portraying God without makeup;
>
> Sean Connery revealing that he acted with Michael Caine before *The Man Who Would be King*, in a BBC TV special, *Requiem for a Heavyweight;*
>
> and Dustin Hoffman disclosing problems working with children.

We also, for posterity, added David Niven's last interview, which was recorded a few months before his death.

The broadcast also included snippets from the following guests on the show:

Sydney Pollock, Jack Lemmon, Walter Matthau, Roger Moore, Jessica Lang, Shirley MacLaine, Steve Martin, Peter O'Toole, Albert Finney, Jane Fonda, Jacqueline Bisset, Angelica Huston, James Garner, Sissy Spacek, Bette Midler, Fred MacMurray, Vanessa Redgrave, Charlton Heston, Tom Cruise, Gene Kelly, Julie Andrews, Meryl Streep, Jeremy Irons, Harrison Ford, Milos Forman, Tom Hulce, and Kris Kristofferson (the latter defending *Heaven's Gate*! – the film which brought United Artists to its knees).

The show was so popular that we created more specials of "the best interviews" another eight times. This was in addition to our regular shows, which later included Barbra Streisand, Clint Eastwood, Peter O'Toole, and others.

Another guest whom I recall vividly was Mervyn LeRoy, a legend in Tinseltown and creator of such wonderful films as *Wizard of Oz, Blossoms in the Dust, Random Harvest*, and so on. He was bemoaning the fact that he had not directed a film in three years and couldn't secure any job in Hollywood. I questioned him on the subject of the script he was trying to get financed before adding "Mervyn you are worth 100 million dollars," and before I could finish the sentence he said "one hundred and twenty-five million." I continued with "Then why don't you spend ten million and show Hollywood that you still have the talent?"

His succinct reply was "ME – SPEND MY OWN MONEY – ARE YOU CRAZY?"

In conclusion, I must say that I will never forget the late Jerry Harvey, who was the genius behind the films we selected for the show. His encyclopaedic knowledge of almost every motion picture made in America was outstanding. He approached me on one occasion to enquire if I knew of any movie that starred Spencer Tracy and Humphrey Bogart. When I returned a blank stare, he told me that he had booked the film, a 1930 Fox feature *Up the River*. How he obtained this rare classic remained a mystery up to his death.

After the channel's demise, a documentary called *Z Channel – A Magnificent Obsession* was created by Xan Cassavetes. Its launch was at the Cannes Film Festival and it really demonstrated Jerry Harvey's genius. He discovered so many features that were thought lost, and at the same time assisted in the airing of European products that would otherwise have been overlooked.

SUMMING UP

A PUBLICIST'S JOB IS A CURIOUS ONE. It is to gain as much media exposure as possible for a client, or product, yet he/she remains totally anonymous. When a campaign goes well, people think it has happened by itself. The publicist is rarely, if ever, credited or mentioned. Of course, when something doesn't go so well, then the publicist gets blamed!

What one learns quickly in Hollywood is that there is no logic. Nobody knows anything!

So how does a publicist, so anonymous in this world, get work and clients? Well, the only opportunities one has are contacting agents, business managers, lawyers, etc. of the talent, or contact the person directly. Non-return phone calls are common place! As a result, one has to survive by being somewhat aggressive and using personal contacts. Often clients and friends will make personal recommendations, which is wonderful.

If I have one failing, it is in not having a great ego to publicize myself. I have always thought that the client is paying for publicity and it is he or she that should appear in stories. There are of course one or two publicists who like nothing better than the sound of their own voice, or the sight of themselves on TV. Who are they really working for I ask?

I have been blessed in life, in love, and in my career. As a boy, I escaped the "real world" in the picture palaces of London. I dreamed about one day being in Hollywood. Of course, a lot of hard work has gone into me getting here, and staying here, but along the way I have had terrific fun.

As I said right at the beginning, I haven't set out to "dish the dirt" or give away any secrets, as that would be commercial suicide for one thing; and I am not that sort of person anyway. I simply wanted to share some of my experiences, good and bad, and to give a little insight into a particular aspect of Hollywood.

I hope you have enjoyed it as much as I have enjoyed recalling it all.

ACKNOWLEDGEMENTS

THANKS MUST FIRSTLY GO to Gareth Owen, who has taken my ramblings, notes, and observations, and translated them into readable English. Also, to our proof reader Iris Harwood for keeping us on the straight and narrow.

As is always the case, a book is not just the result of one person – no matter what they say! I have many people to thank for giving me the material on which to write these memoirs: the producers, directors, stars, studio heads, friends, and most importantly, my wife Janice who took me "for better or worse" over thirty years ago. At times it must have felt like I spent days, weeks, and months away from home, and then I burned the midnight oil researching material when I *was* at home. However, I couldn't have achieved a fraction of what I have without her, her patience, and her love.

The entertainment business is notoriously difficult to carve out a career in, but with enthusiasm and a little luck one can make it, and survive in it. I'm proof of that.

I dedicate this book all those who have encouraged me to share my memories. They all deserve my heartfelt thanks for accompanying me on the road I have travelled, including those who have since gone to their great reward. I sincerely hope nobody will be offended by their absence.

Lightning Source UK Ltd.
Milton Keynes UK
UKHW022159270223
417761UK00005B/437